TEACHING
INFORMATION LITERACY
THRESHOLD CONCEPTS:
Lesson Plans for Librarians

Edited by
Patricia Bravender
Hazel McClure
Gayle Schaub

Association of College and Research Libraries

A division of the American Library Association

Chicago, Illinois 2015

The paper used in this publication meets the minimum requirements of American National Standard for Information Sciences–Permanence of Paper for Printed Library Materials, ANSI Z39.48-1992. ∞

Library of Congress Cataloging-in-Publication Data

Teaching information literacy threshold concepts : lesson plans for librarians / edited by Patricia Bravender, Hazel McClure, Gayle Schaub.
    pages cm
 ISBN 978-0-8389-8771-1 (pbk.) -- ISBN 978-0-8389-8772-8 (pdf) -- ISBN 978-0-8389-8773-5 (epub) -- ISBN 978-0-8389-8774-2 (kindle) 1. Information literacy--Study and teaching (Higher) 2. Research--Methodology--Study and teaching (Higher) 3. Communication in learning and scholarship. 4. Library orientation for college students. I. Bravender, Patricia. II. McClure, Hazel Anne. III. Schaub, Gayle.
 ZA3075.T434 2015
 028.7071'173--dc23
                        2015015254

Printed in the United States of America.
19 18 17 16 15 5 4 3 2

Table of Contents

Editors' Preface

THIS BOOK BEGAN with a conversation.

Always interested in trying something new and meaningful to help students in our disciplines, we often find ourselves hunkering down with each other or other colleagues before or after class sessions to share or solicit ideas about what worked, what might work, or what didn't work. Our university library is no different than most in that we and our colleagues came to this profession from a variety of previous careers and backgrounds. We also have varying levels of teaching experience. Our class session debriefings help us learn from our successes and failures, providing us with valuable insights and ideas for future lessons. One day in the summer of 2012, the topic of lesson plans came up along with the issue of how to best to use the small amount of time we have in class. We don't teach credit-bearing classes, and we often are asked to teach to a specific research assignment created by a professor. We are guests in someone else's classroom. We discussed ways to develop lesson plans that would allow us to teach the concepts of information literacy in ways that would be interesting to students and meaningful to professors, rather than just teaching the mechanics of searching.

Patricia described a workshop she attended where the theory of *threshold concepts* was mentioned. The idea that there could be foundational and transformative concepts in information literacy was profoundly memorable for Patricia and clicked immediately with Gayle and Hazel. It was exactly how we wanted to approach our instruction: focusing on the concepts, the *whys* of information and research, rather than the *hows*. Before we knew anything about the revision of the Association of College and Research Libraries *Information Literacy Standards for Higher Education*,[1] we began our own process of identifying what we believed to be the threshold concepts in information literacy as a way to better inform our lesson plan creation and development. Using Meyer and Land's theory of threshold concepts,[2] we examined our university's *Information Literacy Core Competencies*,[3] identifying what we saw as the fundamental concepts—the basic ideas students should understand to be truly information literate—and finding the ways that the concepts of information literacy resonate with the skills of information literacy. Our goal at that point was simple. We wanted to find out what students *really* need to know so that we could set about figuring out how best to teach just that.

Along the way in our concept-finding mission, we discovered the work of Townsend, Hofer and Brunetti.[4] We recognized that our ideas looked, perhaps not so surprisingly, remarkably similar to theirs. For instance, one threshold concept we identified was that the process of information creation determines its rank, value, cost, and possible bias. In our findings, we articulated the importance of the process behind the production and creation of information over its packaging. Though we didn't formally name this concept, we found it aligned with Townsend, Brunetti, and Hofer's concept, *Format as Process*.[5] It was exciting to have our work confirmed by virtue of its alignment with others' large scale efforts. The idea that there are basic concepts that are core to information literacy was reinforced by the fact that numbers of information professionals were coming separately to the same conclusions. We recognized the potential value in creating, locating, and compiling a collection of lesson plans directed at teaching these concepts. It was clear to us that we weren't the only ones interested in doing so. A book of lesson plans created by librarians, for librarians seemed a great way to share what we were learning and to learn from others.

The release of the draft *ACRL Framework for Information Literacy for Higher Education*[6] in 2014 introduced threshold concepts to librarians everywhere. We were excited to witness and join in this new conversation about conceptual information literacy instruction. What we heard from many was uncertainty about how to teach *ideas*. The concepts, as laid out in the *Framework*, are meant as just that—a conceptual framework. They require us to come up with ways to communicate them to students. In the comments of instruction librarians teaching everything from single sessions to semester-long courses, we recognized the need for practical materials to help transform student understanding. It seemed that we were not the only ones looking for meaningful information literacy content for our instruction.

Like the document that preceded it, the *Framework* and the frames therein will serve as a guide for academic librarianship and will in future decades be reevaluated and revised. It is dynamic, a work in progress. The same is true of threshold concept research and, we hope, the work we have done in this book. We identified more than six threshold concepts, but we include and describe in this book only those used in the January 2015 *Framework*.[7] We realize the potential for additional threshold concepts, including but not limited to *information as a human right* and *every discipline uses a distinct discourse*. It is our intention that instruction librarians use the lessons within the specific contexts of their own classes. It is our hope that the contributions of so many librarians contained within these pages offer ideas and inspiration for others to use, adapt, share, and transform into more ideas for practical applications of threshold concepts in the classroom.

Many instruction librarians have the good fortune of being able to learn in a wide variety of ways: from mentors, colleagues in our own libraries and in professional associations, experience, professional development opportunities, and the scholarship that is currently being contributed to the field on information literacy threshold concepts. However, some academic librarians have had little formal education about pedagogy. Finding ways to impart a set of skills and abilities to students or to facilitate the understanding of foundational information literacy concepts can seem like a tall order. Both are necessary yet can be a challenge for librarians who must enter the classroom and put ideas into practice.

This book, compiled with the insights, wisdom, and dedication of teaching librarians from a range of institutions, is an effort to contribute to the conversation and empower teaching librarians to meet the challenge. The lessons offered here are suggestions for ways to put theory into practice in order to help our students' transformation into information literate individuals.

NOTES

1. "Standards for Libraries in Higher Education." American Library Association, August 29, 2006. http://www.ala.org/acrl/standards/standardslibraries.
2. Meyer, Jan and Ray Land. "Threshold Concepts and Troublesome Knowledge: Linkages to Ways of Thinking and Practising with the Disciplines. ETL Project Occasional Report 4." Edinburgh: Enhancing Teaching-Learning Environments in Undergraduate Courses Project, (May 2003): 1.
3. "Information Literacy Core Competencies." Grand Valley State University Libraries, March 18, 2010. http://gvsu.edu/library/information-literacy-core-competencies-168.htm.
4. Townsend, Lori, Korey Brunetti, and Amy R. Hofer. "Threshold Concepts and Information Literacy." *portal : Libraries and the Academy* 11, no. 3, (2011): 853–869.
5. Ibid, 861.
6. Information Literacy Competency Standards for Higher Education Task Force. "Framework for Information Literacy for Higher Education, Draft 1." Chicago: Association of College and Research Libraries, February 20, 2014. http://acrl.ala.org/ilstandards/wp-content/uploads/2014/02/Framework-for-IL-for-HE-Draft-1-Part-1.pdf.
7. Information Literacy Competency Standards for Higher Education Task Force. "Framework for Information Literacy for Higher Education, Final Draft." Chicago: Association of College and Research Libraries, January 16, 2015, http://acrl.ala.org/ilstandards/wp-content/uploads/2015/01/Framework-MW15-Board-Docs.pdf.

ACKNOWLEDGMENTS

Thank you to the librarians who answered our call for submissions and who have been teaching information literacy threshold concepts in creative and interesting ways, spurring us to new understanding and approaches. Thanks also to our Grand Valley State University colleagues, particularly our teaching team (you know who you are) and other Research and Instruction Librarians, with whom we debated and learned and grew in our understanding of the threshold concepts. We are grateful to Lori Townsend, whose comments helped clarify our thinking, Anna Dorsey for her graphic design contributions, and Cara Cadena, who proofread and gave us valuable feedback. Additional thanks go to all who attended our

Michigan Library Association Academic Libraries Conference presentation, asked great questions, and shared their ideas with us. A huge thank you to our friendly editor, Kathryn Deiss who kept us going, gave great advice, and was continually supportive. We extend our final thanks to the creators of the ACRL Framework and all of the librarians across the country who weighed in on its development and shared their ideas and opinions publicly. We're deeply grateful for the conversation.

Gayle Schaub, Hazel McClure and Patricia Bravender
November 2014

Introduction

WHEN THE FIRST part of the first draft of the *Framework for Information Literacy in Higher Education* was released by the Association of College and Research Libraries (ACRL) in February 2014, the very idea of threshold concepts was new to many librarians, particularly the idea of using them to teach information literacy. But, in fact, the identification of threshold concepts within disciplines of knowledge had its beginnings more than a decade prior to this. Since then, the study of the nature of threshold concepts and their identification in different disciplines has been a topic of research by scholars in many academic fields of study.

THRESHOLD CONCEPTS

Jan Meyer and Ray Land, early scholars of threshold concept theory, have published extensively about this way of looking at learning in disciplines. According to Meyer and Land:

> [a] threshold concept can be considered akin to a portal, opening up a new and previously inaccessible way of thinking about something. It represents a transformed way of understanding, or interpreting, or viewing something without which the learner cannot progress.[1]

Meyer and Land describe threshold concepts as likely to have the following characteristics:

- Threshold concepts are **transformative.** They change how a student views an idea or discipline. For example, once a student has internalized the concept that scholarship is a conversation, she or he will understand a scholarly article not as a stand-alone document in a database, but instead as just one voice in an ongoing, dynamic conversation. As a result, the way that the student does research will also be transformed.
- Threshold concepts are also probably **irreversible.** It is very difficult or possibly impossible to unlearn these foundational concepts.
- Threshold concepts are **integrative**, in that they may help a student understand how parts of a body of knowledge are related in ways that they previously didn't understand.
- Threshold concepts are possibly **bounded** within a discipline or area of knowledge. They may help define the edges of that discipline.
- Threshold concepts are often **troublesome**, meaning the knowledge gained may not be intuitive and may appear to contradict a student's previously held opinions or understanding. Threshold concepts may also be so new to the student that s/he may have trouble grasping them.[2]

Since the introduction of threshold concepts, scholars have studied their application in their own disciplines, including computer science, engineering, biology, and economics.

THRESHOLD CONCEPTS IN INFORMATION LITERACY

Some of the earliest identification of threshold concepts specific to the field of information literacy was presented and written by Lori Townsend, Korey Brunetti, and Amy R. Hofer.[3] Work done before this posited information literacy as either a threshold concept itself, reaching across the disciplines, or inclusive of ideas from a wider sphere of behavioral or emotional content.[4] Identifying the transformative ideas paved a way to addressing the *whys* of information literacy so that librarians might help students make sense of finding and using information. Threshold concepts enable students to have a true understanding of the information landscape that extends beyond the structure and jargon of a particular time or place.

Some of the characteristics of these threshold concepts are relatively straightforward. They are transformational, irreversible, and bounded. They change the way a student understands disciplinary content, its discourse, and practices, and that understanding is highly unlikely to undo itself. One characteristic that is less straightforward is the idea of troublesome knowledge. Librarians (or any educators, for that matter) can't know what previous knowledge or preconceptions students bring with them to class. Students may struggle with different concepts at different points for any number of reasons. Teaching with threshold concepts is a more student-centered approach in that it asks the librarian to recognize the potential troublesome knowledge.

In the last three years, the discussion of a threshold-concept approach to information literacy instruction has taken off. This approach offers librarians a way to engage students with core ideas rather than step-by-step demonstration instruction. Librarians face the same challenges in higher education as content faculty. We search for the best methods to facilitate the many ways we refer to applied learning: critical thinking, problem solving, 21st century skills, lifelong learning. Yet, often, with little formal instructional training, librarians may rely on practices that don't always encourage a conceptual understanding of information literacy. Threshold concepts provide this foundation. Librarians can use them as a way to recognize their own best practices and build on them to create single-session lessons or semester-long classes, or to integrate information literacy into the curricula of disciplines across campus.

MOVING FORWARD: THEORY INTO PRACTICE

The Information Literacy Competency Standards for Higher Education were adopted by the Association of College and Research Libraries in 2000. Most librarians are familiar and comfortable with their understanding of these standards, which identify a number of skills and abilities that college students should develop in order to be considered information literate. Colleges and universities have used these standards as a way to promote and integrate information literacy into their curricula. In June 2012, the ACRL board approved a recommendation that these standards be revised to reflect the shifts in the higher education landscape since their adoption in 2000. A task force was created to revise the standards, and they created a draft of a new document, called The Framework for Information Literacy for Higher Education, which has been shared with academic librarians.

The Task Force released several drafts of the *Framework* between February 2014 and January 2015.[5] These documents represented a major departure from the 2000 standards in both theory and content. The January 2015 *Framework* filed[6] by ACRL offers a set of six frames that employ recent research in information literacy threshold concepts. They are

1. Scholarship as Conversation
2. Research as Inquiry
3. Authority is Constructed and Contextual
4. Information Creation as a Process
5. Searching as Strategic Exploration
6. Information has Value

For more discussion of threshold concepts and their relationship to the *Framework*, see the *Framework* itself, which is valuable not only for its inclusion of threshold concepts, but also for its use of the idea of metaliteracy and the incorporation of knowledge practices and dispositions into each frame.

There has been and will continue to be debate and discussion surrounding the theory of threshold concepts in general and the identification of threshold concepts in information literacy in particular. The threshold concepts inspiring the work of the ACRL frames have been debated and edited over time, and serve as the organizing factor behind this book. (Each chapter is organized around a threshold concept that supports one of the frames and we have included an introduction to each threshold concept in each chapter.) However, it is possible that there are other information literacy threshold concepts that haven't been identified yet, or that may resonate more strongly for different purposes or in different disciplinary research. The readers of this book are encouraged to consider for themselves and their students whether there are other underlying concepts that would transform student understanding of information literacy. The list of threshold concepts may grow or change over time, and it is the knowledge of information literacy, the practical experience, and the expertise of teaching librarians that will inform these changes. We believe that the important element of teaching with information literacy threshold concepts is teaching with a focus on the underlying conceptual understanding rather than focusing on an acquisition of technical ability.

Some librarians who are researching information literacy threshold concepts argue that it's difficult to teach or learn threshold concepts in single class sessions. However, at this time, many teaching librarians do not teach information literacy credit-bearing classes. One way to address this constraint is to work with disciplinary faculty to ensure that the research session is integrated into the course where students are at the point of need. Communicating clearly with course instructors to establish shared goals for both the content they are teaching and the information literacy concepts that the librarian is teaching helps create learning opportunities for students that are timely and relevant to them and their work.

However, not all teaching librarians are asked by disciplinary faculty to come into a classroom multiple times throughout a semester to reinforce these concepts. The reality is that most teaching librarians get "one shot" at any particular class. The lessons in this book were created with flexibility in mind. Most of them are designed for single sessions, but could be adapted and combined to teach longer, more sustained units or courses, either within other disciplinary courses, or in a credit-bearing information literacy course. These lessons, even when used in a single session, help guide teaching librarians to approach these interactions with the conceptual underpinning of research in mind, rather than skills-based demonstrations. They are designed to help students learn the skills they need to do research, but more importantly, to understand *why* we do research, or why we do research in particular ways.

Creating plans for engaging threshold concept-based instructional sessions may be difficult, particularly after being familiar with a focus on teaching *skills*. This book seeks to help meet this challenge by providing detailed, ready-to-use, and easily adaptable lesson ideas for teaching librarians as ways to help students understand and be transformed by information literacy threshold concepts. The lessons in this book, which have been created by teaching librarians across the country, have been written to provide practical and concrete ideas about how to do this. The lessons collected here are categorized according to the six information literacy frames identified in the *Framework for Information Literacy in Higher Education*. Many of these lessons relate to more than one concept. Overlapping concepts are identified in lessons and in a list of Lessons with Overlapping Information Literacy Threshold Concepts at the end of this book.

The approaches outlined in this book and the underlying threshold concepts have the potential to not only guide the teaching of individual lessons or classes, but also to provide a rich ground to enter conversations with faculty. It may be difficult to collaborate with non-librarians about information literacy, with its seemingly endless jargon. Threshold concepts, on the other hand, focus on the underlying understanding of scholarly communication and research; these ideas transcend the borders of information literacy. Using threshold concepts as a way to think about approaching shared goals with disciplinary faculty, librarians can focus not on explaining jargon, but on explaining how the information literacy threshold concepts manifest in disciplines in which their students are working. As a result, librarians can help students build an awareness of the disciplinary conversations and their conventions, and ideally set the stage for students to more fully understand and contribute to the information landscape around them.

HOW TO USE THIS BOOK

These lessons have been designed to be used in their current form, but they can be modified to suit the style and needs of individual librarians and their students. Lessons can be combined for longer classes or several can be given over the course of a semester to reinforce learning or introduce new threshold concepts. Examples of suggested handouts or worksheets are provided in the Appendix. Full-size handouts are available online at www.ala.org/acrl/files/handouts.pdf

The editors introduce each lesson with a brief summary, followed by a more detailed explanation of how the lesson specifically addresses the threshold concept or concepts. This section, called *Concept in Context*, puts the threshold concept into the specific context of an individual lesson. Information literacy threshold concepts can be a challenge to understand and to teach, and using individual lessons through which to approach the larger ideas offers librarians a way to take on these concepts and help students build toward an understanding of them. With these short contextualizations, the editors articulate the *why* of the lesson—how it gets at the concept in question or provides an introduction to the idea.

The lessons have been formatted in a lesson design inspired by Madeline Hunter and Doug Russell called *Instruction Theory Into Practice*, commonly called an ITIP.[7] Hunter was a strong proponent of the idea that one of the most influential factors in successful teaching was skill in planning the instruction session.[8] Many librarians find the process of writing lesson plans to be helpful in planning information literacy instruction by identifying and focusing on learning goals. Written plans are also an effective way to share ideas with other librarians.

The plans in this book contain basic elements that include Learning Goals, Anticipatory Set, Lesson Objectives, Input/Modeling, Check for Understanding, Guided Practice, and Independent Practice. Not every element is necessary or appropriate for every lesson, and some of the lessons in this book do not include every element. Users of these plans are encouraged to modify and adapt them for their own needs by determining which elements are appropriate for their own classes and in what order they are given. Each librarian can decide which elements should be included, excluded, or combined as they consider their own learning goals and objectives and the needs of their students.

This book departs from Hunter's ITIP format in that Learning Goals replace Learning Objectives. Objectives are measurable, and in these lessons it would be difficult, if not impossible, to apply a standard measure for learning in such a variety of contexts and classrooms. Librarians may create learning objectives that are appropriate for their own interpretations of these lessons within their classes. In addition, we encourage instruction librarians to use the Guided Practice and Check for Understanding elements of the format to work with faculty in gauging the understanding of students beyond the completion of session or series of sessions.

ELEMENTS OF THE LESSON PLANS

Learning Goals are the intended learning outcomes of a lesson. Learning goals are not necessarily measurable, but rather are the eventual learning aims as determined by the author of the lesson. These goals are usually not communicated to the students. Also, there is usually no need to explicitly identify to the students what threshold concept is being addressed unless doing so is an essential part of the lesson.

The **Anticipatory Set** draws students into the lesson, engaging them with the content and catching their attention. It can be a question to elicit student response, a story to pique their interest, or a short activity that involves them in the problem or issue at hand. This element sets the stage or provides context by tapping into students' prior knowledge or experience. It can be especially useful for librarians who have had limited or no contact with the students prior to the class session. This set can help build rapport with students as well.

The **Lesson Objective Stated** is communicating to the students what they will be learning, how it will help them, and why it matters. It should explain to students what the librarian wants them to learn or understand and signal what is important to focus on.

Input is the method used to deliver the information to the students. **Modeling**, which is the librarian performing the activity him or herself while explaining to the students what he/she is doing, is often part of this input.

During a **Check for Understanding** the librarian elicits signs as to whether students possess the information or skill being taught. This is a tall order when trying to teach information literacy threshold concepts. This checking is frequently done as part of **Guided Practice**. Many of the lessons in this book ask students to engage in active learning exercises of some kind to help cement the learning goals. Through observation of students during this guided practice, the librarian can begin to assess whether students are beginning to understand the main idea of the lesson and the threshold concept that it addresses.

During **Independent Practice** students practice the new skill or process with little or no librarian direction. This is often in the form of an in-class exercise or an assignment.

Often, the independent practice is linked with an assignment that students are doing in the class that the librarian is visiting. It may be possible, in these cases, to work with faculty members to assess the effectiveness of the lesson after the library session.

NOTES

1. Jan Meyer and Ray Land, *Threshold Concepts and Troublesome Knowledge: Linkages to Ways of Thinking and Practising with the Disciplines*. (Edinburgh: ETL Project, Universities of Edinburgh, Coventry and Durham, 2003).

2. Ibid.

3. Lori Townsend, Korey Brunetti, and Amy R. Hofer. "Threshold Concepts and Information Literacy." *portal : Libraries and the Academy* 11, no. 3, (2011): 853–869.

4. Margaret Blackmore, "Student Engagement with Information: Applying a Threshold Concept Approach to Information Literacy Development," paper presented at the 3rd Biennial Threshold Concepts Symposium: Exploring Transformative Dimensions of Threshold Concepts, Sydney, Australia 1-2 July 2010.

5. Information Literacy Competency Standards for Higher Education Task Force. "Framework for Information Literacy for Higher Education, Final Draft." Chicago: Association of College and Research Libraries, January 16, 2015. http://acrl.ala.org/ilstandards/wp-content/uploads/2015/01/Framework-MW15-Board-Docs.pdf.

6. The official action of 'filing' the *Framework* is described in greater detail in "More from the ACRL Board on the Framework for Information Literacy for Higher Education," *The ACRL Insider,* February 4, 2015. http://www.acrl.ala.org/acrlinsider/archives/category/information-literacy.

7. This theory was introduced by Madeline Hunter and Doug Russell in "Planning for Effective Instruction." *Instructor* (September, 1977): 4–12; reprinted in Hunter, Madeline. *Enhancing Teaching*, 1994: 87–97. New York: Macmillan College Publishing Co.

8. Ibid, 87.

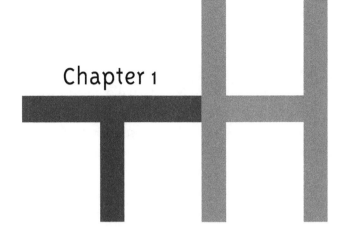

Chapter 1

Scholarship as Conversation

NO IDEA STANDS alone, whether it appears in the most prestigious scholarly journal or flits across the screen in 140 characters or less. Each argument, observation, discovery, or criticism in a discipline or about a problem depends upon and sometimes competes with countless thoughts or communications before it. Like those in a town hall meeting or a comment section on a blog post, the voices in the conversation are often arguing, agreeing, contributing related but tangential information, analyzing, and raising new questions. The threshold concept of *Scholarship as Conversation* addresses this interplay and the way scholars use it. Librarians can help students learn to identify the threads of these conversations and navigate the often confusing information contexts.

The *Framework for Information Literacy for Higher Education* defines *Scholarship as Conversation* as "[c]ommunities of scholars, researchers, or professionals engage in sustained discourse with new insights and discoveries occurring over time as a result of varied perspectives and interpretations."[1] Novices in scholarship or in a discipline will not immediately grasp the nature of the complex, sometimes contradictory nature of a body of conversant texts. It should be noted that not all participants in the conversations are interacting through *written* texts; sometimes the conversation plays out in podcasts, radio broadcasts, or even via art objects. When given an assignment that requires research, a student may seek out a single text or set of texts that support his or her beliefs or preexisting opinions about a topic. However, to truly seek a solution to a problem, or an answer to a question, information seekers need to find, read (or watch), interpret, and understand more than one piece of information; they need to understand that each is just one voice of many within a larger scholarly conversation.

Knowing that a single document may be created as a reaction to or as an elaboration of other ideas and arguments, students can understand more than the content of that individual document. They can begin to understand the *context* in which the ideas are being presented, and, as a result, can learn more about the problem, the conversation, the discipline, and scholarly research itself. Navigating the conversation and knowing that sometimes there is no one right answer is a huge part of "getting" this threshold concept.

It is also important to note that the same topic may be approached in different ways within different disciplines, and that there are distinct "conversations" within each discipline. When finding the most complete information, consulting the concurrent conversations can be eye opening. The idea that research raises questions as well as answers them is one that arises in another threshold concept, *Research as Inquiry*. Students must be aware of the various voices and threads of disciplinary conversations in order to find their own way in.

This book presents a variety of approaches to guide students to an understanding of some of these ideas. In Andrea Baer's lesson, "The Conversational Nature of Sources of Information," students are asked to examine two articles, one of which is a response to the other. This demonstrates the interplay of two viewpoints. In Brandon West's lesson, students use a particular form of scholarly communication, blog posts, to enter the conversation and gain some understanding of the topic before delving into scholarly literature. In "Mapping Scholarly Conversations" by Kate Langan, students are prompted to create a conceptual map of what they already know about a topic, add to that map by doing pre-research, and then research. This allows students to visualize the relationships between different conversants and ideas surrounding the topics, giving them an entry point for their own contributions. This chapter includes other approaches for librarians to use to help students understand this essential concept.

Scholarship as Conversation is closely related to the other information literacy threshold concepts. The threshold concept of *Information Creation as a Process* is concerned with understanding the processes behind format and thus understanding more fully the purpose and uses of information. Scholarly conversations play out via published communications, and these publications range in form and delivery. The ways in which information consumers interact with the pieces of the scholarly conversation change as advancing technology affects the modes of communication. However, throughout these changes in format, the conversation remains. Another potentially overlapping threshold concept is that of *Authority is Constructed and Contextual.* This is important in grasping the conversation as a whole, and authority can be more fully analyzed if one has a good understanding of the scholarly conversation as a whole.

Throughout this book, the threshold concept of *Scholarship as Conversation* manifests in lessons for other threshold concepts. To learn more, consult the list of lessons with overlapping threshold concepts.

NOTES

1.   Information Literacy Competency Standards for Higher Education Task Force, *Framework for Information Literacy for Higher Education, Final Draft"* (Chicago: Association of College and Research Libraries, January 16, 2015A: 10). http://acrl.ala.org/ilstandards/wp-content/uploads/2015/01/Framework-MW15-Board-Docs.pdf.

The Conversational Nature of Sources of Information

Students are asked to examine two magazine articles that are different parts of a larger, more complex conversation.

CONCEPT IN CONTEXT

This lesson introduces students to the idea that scholarship is a conversation. Students are introduced to two articles, one of which is a rebuttal to the other. In the rebuttal, the author references other articles and sources of information, expanding the conversation to include additional voices. In reading contrasting viewpoints and examining the textual evidence the authors use to support their positions, the students get a sense for the practice of formulating and supporting an argument. They learn that this "conversation" between scholars is informed over time, drawing on the work of previous conversation participants. Importantly, this lesson also shows students that in order to contribute to any scholarly conversation in a meaningful way, they need to look for multiple views on a topic, including those that do not mirror their own.

Author: Andrea Baer, Undergraduate Education Librarian
         Indiana University, Bloomington, Indiana

Level: Intermediate to advanced

Estimated Time: The activity described under Input/Modeling will require varying amounts of time, depending on the sources assigned. However, it can be introduced prior to class and completed outside of class time. The remainder of the lesson requires approximately 35–45 minutes.

The examples given here are relatively short magazine articles that can be freely accessed online. Because of the articles' length, most students should be able to read them at the beginning of a class session, allowing for the entire lesson to be conducted in a standard hour or in one hour and fifteen minutes. Alternately, the librarian may choose to select longer, scholarly articles and have students read the articles prior to coming to class.

MATERIALS NEEDED

- Computers with Internet access
- Handout for the Input/Modeling activity that includes:
  a. citations of the assigned sources
  b. list of source characteristics to be analyzed (See Input/ Modeling section, Part 1 and Part 2)

  See Appendix or www.ala.org/acrl/files/handouts.pdf

LEARNING GOALS

- Students will identify how scholars use information to influence their own scholarly work.
- Students will recognize information sources as conversational and dialogic in nature.
- Students will apply a dialogic approach to evaluating sources.

ANTICIPATORY SET

Librarian Script: "When we encounter information out of context, it can be difficult to see how that information is meaningful. All pieces of information, however, are products of larger conversations. We can therefore think about sources as snippets of these bigger discussions."

"When we examine one piece of information, we often find that it references many other sources of information. Similarly, when we do research, we are listening in on many different dialogues, which may happen in different contexts (and not just in written form). As researchers, our challenging (and fun) work is to piece together those different conversational strands, to think about how they fit together, and to consider how we will enter into and add to the conversation."

LESSON OBJECTIVE STATED

Librarian Script: "Today we will consider how sources (such as journal articles, books, websites) can be understood as part of a larger dialogue. In doing this, we will identify how authors and speakers use other sources to support their own ideas. Finally, we will consider how we can evaluate a source based on the supporting evidence that the author uses from other sources. Evaluating sources can also help us think about how we use sources for our own purposes, such as persuading or making an argument."

INPUT/MODELING

This lesson begins with a pre-instruction activity that can be completed prior to or during class. Students read two brief articles or article excerpts that reflect varying viewpoints on a course-related topic. In order to emphasize the conversational nature of sources, the librarian might choose one article that explicitly references the other or two sources that allude to each other. For example, an article written in the *National Review Online* challenges a claim made in an earlier article printed in the *Rolling Stone*. (See citations below.) Comparing the views expressed in these two articles can start a conversation about audience, purpose, bias, or rhetorical conventions employed in various publications. If these examples are used, it is important to tell students that the Richwine article in *National Review* references and links to an earlier article Richwine posted at the Heritage Foundation website that contains a number of other references.

> Matt Taibbi, "Ripping Off Young America: The College-Loan Scandal," *Rolling Stone*, August 15, 2013, http://www.rolling-stone.com/politics/news/ripping-off-young-america-the-college-loan-scandal-20130815

> Jason Richwine, "What 'Profits'? Rolling Stone's Matt Taibbi Misunderstands Student Loans," *National Review Online*, August 23, 2013, http://www.nationalreview.com/corner/356551/what-profits-rolling-stones-matt-taibbi-misunderstands-student-loans-jason-richwine

The librarian should explain to students that they will be considering the rhetorical context of both sources (e.g., audience, purpose, genre, and bias) as well as the relationships between the sources. Students should be prepared to support their answers with details from the sources; annotating key parts of the sources may help them develop their answers.

Part 1: For each source, students will identify:

a. the publication source, as well as the publication's general audience and purpose (The librarian may provide tips on how to determine intended audience and purpose, such as reviewing other content in the publication, reading the publication's self-description, or examining certain stylistic features, visual elements, or writing conventions.)

b. the source's general purpose (e.g., to inform, to make an argument)

c. the source's central message or argument

d. one or two pieces of supporting evidence used to convey the central message or argument

Part 2: Finally, students will note a strong connection between the two sources which brings them into dialogue with one another.

GUIDED PRACTICE/CHECK FOR UNDERSTANDING

The above pre-instruction activity sets the stage for class discussions in large and small groups. While Parts 1a-c of the activity may be addressed more briefly as an entire class, students may benefit from both large and small group discussion for Part 1d and Part 2.

For Parts 1a–c, the class discusses and agrees upon answers. (Throughout this exchange the librarian can highlight ways to understand sources in conversational terms.)

During discussion of Part 1d, the librarian addresses the fact that evidence used in sources often comes from additional sources (which reflect additional pieces of a larger dialogue). Students will be asked to provide one example of supporting evidence used in one of the articles and, as a class, will be asked to assess the relevance and credibility of this evidence. This may become an opportunity to discuss source verification and citation. For example, are students able to identify and locate the sources from which the evidence comes? What does the practice of citation, or its absence, suggest about the sources or about the rhetorical conventions used by the author(s)?

Next the students work in pairs or groups of three, identifying in each source one piece of supporting evidence and evaluating that evidence in terms of its relevance and credibility. Students should be prepared to share their examples with the entire class. After small group discussions, the class may share and discuss their examples and evaluation of each source's use of evidence.

Part 2 (the connection between the two sources) can be structured similarly to Part 1. First the librarian conducts a large class discussion shaped by student responses, then asks students to work in small groups, and finally brings the class back together for another large class discussion. At the beginning of discussion the librarian can state that there are often multiple connections between sources, so students may have various answers.

To further acknowledge the legitimacy of students' having varying answers, the librarian can note that different audience members may be more drawn to certain aspects of the sources than to other aspects. Part of understanding information sources as conversational involves viewing ourselves as audiences, researchers, and potential contributors to that dialogue. Conversations in class during this lesson are yet another example of how engagement with sources can be understood as conversational and contextual and shaped by the given rhetorical situation.

Using Information as a Springboard to Research

In this lesson, students use a single article, created for a general/popular audience, as a starting point to a) consider the conversation surrounding this topic and b) consider and discover related topics and disciplines.

CONCEPT IN CONTEXT

This lesson provides students with an accessible entry point to a conversation that includes both scholarly and popular information sources. If we imagine conversation around any given topic as an iceberg, the article that is introduced to students in this lesson might serve as the portion that is visible above the waterline; hidden behind it is a vast and hefty conversation. It is not usually necessary or possible for beginning students to grasp the entire conversation. Instead, they should understand that individual conversational voices (like an NPR article) are connected to other pieces of information, albeit in sometimes indirect and often contradictory ways. These voices can be speaking at different registers, too, for different audiences. Providing students with a single information artifact can let them first grasp the meaning of the article, then build on their understanding and knowledge.

Overlapping Threshold Concept: This lesson also addresses the concept *Searching as Strategic Exploration*.

Authors: Emily Frigo, First Year Initiatives Coordinator

Jessalyn Richter, Writing Instructor
Grand Valley State University, Allendale, Michigan

Level: Basic
Estimated Time: 50–60 minutes

MATERIALS NEEDED

- Computers for students to apply and practice skills presented, although this lesson is adaptable to low-tech classrooms
- Copies of article or URL for article, distributed in the previous class session

- Instructor computer and projector
- Worksheets, which are distributed in previous class session (*see Appendix or www.ala.org/acrl/files/handouts.pdf*)

LEARNING GOALS

- Students will understand that conversations around topics are complex and include both scholarly and non-scholarly pieces of information.
- Students will be able to use a news article as an inspiration/ springboard to find related information on a topic.
- Students will understand a single source of information as part of a larger conversation that can be approached from many disciplinary angles.

ANTICIPATORY SET

The students are given an assignment before class to read an article. Frigo and Richter suggest an NPR article entitled "Nail Biting: Mental Disorder Or Just A Bad Habit?"[1] (Other articles may lend themselves well to this assignment. Such articles should be intended for a popular audience, but must relate to bodies of research from several disciplines.) Students are also are asked to complete a worksheet to prepare for group work and in-class discussion (*see Appendix or www.ala.org/acrl/files/handouts.pdf*).

To frame discussion of the article and engage students, the librarian begins the class by asking who in the class has a bad habit. The students are then asked if they can imagine writing an article about their own bad habit. In the ensuing discussion, connections between the bad habit and possible areas of research (such as the business of habit cessation or the psychology of the causes of bad habits) can be made that set the stage for students to think about how a seemingly mundane topic can lead to research, both on the part of a scholar and a student looking for information.

LESSON OBJECTIVE STATED

Librarian Script: "Today we will be using the following outline in order to learn how an article relates to scholarly conversation and how to use that article to find other sources." [The librarian writes this on the board or projects it for students to see.]

- Part 1: Evaluating the content of the article
- Part 2: Springboard: How to use your source as a stepping stone to find more information
- Part 3: Searching in select databases/discovery tools
- Part 4: Hands-on time for searching your topics

INPUT/MODELING

In small groups, students first review the content of the news article they read, using the following worksheet questions (*see Appendix or www.ala. org/acrl/files/handouts.pdf for full worksheet*).

1. Briefly summarize the article. What interest or question does the author have, what sort of data or evidence does s/he acquire, and what major conclusions (if any) does s/he reach?
2. Was the article written to persuade, propose a solution, give general information, etc.? What was the purpose of the article?
3. Who is the audience?
4. Who is the author/s? Is s/he an expert?
5. What newspaper or journal is the article from? Does it contain any bias that you can identify?
6. What is the date of the article? Is it current? Is currency important to this topic?

Students are asked to briefly report out about article content.

Then, students return to the small group discussion to review the article and to discuss the following questions that are displayed on a screen or given as handouts:

- List some of the main ideas or key concepts. Think of synonyms and brainstorm related terms that are broader or narrower in scope.
- What researchers, organizations, universities, etc. are concerned with the problem? Are any research studies mentioned?
- What questions came to your mind after reading the article?
- Which disciplines may be interested in studying/exploring this or related topics?

These questions encourage them to think about the article not just as a piece of information in itself, but also as a tool for finding additional materials and additional angles on the same topic.

At this point, the class discusses the answers to these questions as a group. As students report out, the librarian records the following on the board:

- Related keywords (synonyms, concepts, researchers, organizations)
- Related questions from each group
- Disciplines that may address this topic.

Students are then briefly introduced to a few key library resources, including a discovery tool and a database. The database can be chosen in relation to the disciplines that have been identified in the discussion.

GUIDED PRACTICE/CHECK FOR UNDERSTANDING

Students are instructed to do searches in these tools using the keywords and questions generated through the discussion.

As a final check for understanding, students are asked to report out on what new information sources they have discovered.

INDEPENDENT PRACTICE

- Students are asked to do a quick search using their chosen topics and identify one source (popular or scholarly) they could use for their next assignment.
- For homework in preparation for the next class, students analyze this source, using the questions discussed during the library session.
- In the next lab session, students use the keywords and questions they identified to search for additional sources on their chosen topic.

NOTES

1. Amy Standen, "Nail Biting: Mental Disorder or Just a Bad Habit?" *Shots: Health News from NPR* (blog), October 1, 2012, http://www.npr.org/blogs/health/2012/10/01/161766321/nail-biting-mental-disorder-or-just-a-bad-habit.

Mapping Scholarly Conversation

In this pre-research lesson, students create concept maps for topics that they are considering for research assignments. Creating concept maps allows students to visualize aspects of issues or questions surrounding their topic, thereby helping them transform their initial inquiries into articulate and viable research questions.

CONCEPT IN CONTEXT

Students often select a topic to research without fully considering the complex conversations surrounding it, or they have unrealistic expectations about what information they will find. By using concept mapping as outlined in this lesson, librarians can help students generate a visual representation of their ideas surrounding a research topic. Being cognizant of their existing ideas can help students create a framework around which to build on these ideas. First they can seek the input of peers, then they can incorporate information from experts. This can culminate in a more thoughtful research question and thesis statement for their research assignment. This exercise allows students to map out a conversation and find an entry point for their contribution. Concept mapping helps students articulate the questions that most interest them, which will lead them into their research with focused inquiry.

Overlapping Threshold Concept: This lesson also addresses the concept *Research as Inquiry.*

Author: Kathleen Anne Langan, Humanities Librarian
Western Michigan University, Kalamazoo

Level: Basic
Estimated Time: 25–35 minutes

MATERIALS NEEDED

- White boards, chalk boards, poster-sized sticky notes, paper, or poster board
- Example of concept map (*see Appendix or www.ala.org/acrl/ files/handouts.pdf for example of a concept map*)

LEARNING GOALS

- Students will learn to develop a thoughtful and meaningful research question from a broad topic.
- Students will learn to recognize that a well-thought-out research question facilitates the research and writing process.

ANTICIPATORY SET

In this anticipatory set, the librarian starts the lesson by demonstrating how to create a concept map. The librarian solicits a topic from one of the students. (The concept map can be drawn around any topic but ideally would be advantageous to use one from the assignment at hand.) The librarian then prompts the rest of the class with questions about what they know about the topic, followed by what they want to know or what their hypothesis is, stimulating conversation in the classroom. As students contribute ideas, the librarian creates a concept map on a whiteboard, chalkboard, or overhead projector. After ideas are mapped out, the librarian then asks students how different nodes of the map are related. The librarian can then point how the different branches of the map can be broken down or grouped together into different research questions, depending on the expectations and limitations of the assignment.

LESSON OBJECTIVE STATED

Librarian Script: "Today we'll each develop clear and focused research questions in order to help shape our papers. To do this, we'll create concept maps. A good concept map not only helps you develop a clear research question, it also identifies the structure of the research paper. It can also help you identify specific information you need to look for to support your thesis statement."

INPUT/MODELING

The librarian introduces concept mapping by discussing the features of the concept map s/he has drawn on the board for/with the class. S/he shares other examples if needed (*see Appendix or www.ala.org/acrl/files/handouts.pdf*).

GUIDED PRACTICE

The librarian asks students to either choose their own topic or choose one from a list of examples provided for the purposes of the assignment. Ideally, students work on a topic with which they have a personal connection and one that relates to the current assignment.

The librarian puts students into groups of three. Each student is to 1) spend five minutes sketching an initial concept map with the knowledge/ideas s/he already has, and 2) contribute ideas to the other group members about their topics as they develop their concept map. The emphasis is placed on conversation and the sharing of ideas. A variety of materials can be used for group concept mapping. (See Materials Needed section.) The author has had success using white/chalk boards.

If group work is not optimal, students can individually sketch maps and then work with a partner to explain their map, as well as trade maps, spending a few minutes adding to the other student's map. This is adaptable, but the point is to prompt them to view their topic through another set of eyes and to practice articulating their research question with someone else's knowledge brought into the conversation.

Next, in this *optional* step, students can spend some time doing preliminary research to investigate what other ideas/people/concepts/language might be involved in the larger conversation about their topic. Students are free to use any research tool available to them to explore and discover aspects of the conversation that they were previously unaware of regarding their topic.

After allowing students to investigate for a set amount of time, the librarian asks them to add to/modify their concept maps based on what they found. The librarian can challenge the students to answer how knowing more impacts the original research question or thesis statement, putting emphasis on the evolving nature of scholarly conversation.

After generating ideas, the next step is for students to distill their ideas into one manageable research question that is *most* interesting to them as well as viable for the assignment. The librarian can ask, *What question do you have about these ideas that you would like to investigate?* This question can draw out relationships between facets of students' maps, or can delve into one aspect of a map, emphasizing that one item on a concept map could become the seed for an entirely new concept map or research question. The librarian should also emphasize that not all aspects of a concept map can be or will be treated in one research assignment and that students need to be *selective*. Librarians should also emphasize that this is a preliminary exploration into the topic and that the focus of a research question might change throughout the research process and that this evolution and transformation is an expected part of a scholarly conversation.

Throughout this lesson, the librarian and the instructor circulate among the students to redirect or clarify as needed.

Figure 1.1. Students in groups creating concept

Figure 1.2. Detail of a student's concept

Crafting a Credible Message

By examining different types of information from the viewpoints of both communicator and audience, students learn to recognize categories of information and how they are interlinked.

CONCEPT IN CONTEXT

Students need to acquire at least a basic facility with information resources and finding tools, such as online databases and catalogs, reference materials, and search engines. Understanding when and how to access the proper information is a necessity for successful research. Equally important is the ability to recognize that the information one discovers not only answers questions, it poses new ones. Students often encounter contradictory information. Working through a lesson that considers both the author and the audience of a work, whether it be a journal or article or a blog post, helps students see the interconnectedness of information.

This awareness makes students better information seekers. They understand that to deliver a credible message, they need to find more than just the *easy* information on a topic—the information that confirms a certain viewpoint or already makes sense to them.

Sometimes this additional information comes in the form of empirical evidence or data, sometimes it takes the form of literary criticism, sometimes a newspaper editorial. This lesson aims to show students how to seek, understand, categorize, and better use the information they find. By using information in different contexts and disciplines, students have a better grasp of the terms tossed about in college classrooms, such as primary source, scholarly article, and others.

Overlapping Threshold Concepts: This lesson also addresses the concepts of *Information Creation as a Process* and *Searching as Strategic Exploration.*

Author: Debbie Morrow, Liaison Librarian
              Grand Valley State University, Allendale, Michigan

Level: Basic/general education
Estimated Time: 50–75 minutes

MATERIALS NEEDED

- Small-group worksheets
- Whiteboard and markers
- Worksheet (*see Appendix or www.ala.org/acrl/files/handouts.pdf*)

LEARNING GOALS

- Students will gain awareness of writing as an author communicating to an audience.
- Students will see the relationship of the content they consume to the writing they do.
- Students will be able to identify primary, secondary, and tertiary resources within the context of their research in a discipline and understand why those labels matter.

ANTICIPATORY SET

Optional Quote (can be projected or handed out):

> "Communication is thought of both as an ordinary action and as an extraordinary act. It is ordinary because it is a major human activity that we engage in each day, but it is extraordinary because communicating with others has the capacity to provide social support and comfort, engage others in deliberation and debate on important issues, delight us with stories and performances, help us understand and manage who we are as people, and manage or resolve conflicts."[1]

Definition of communication is given to class:
A very basic definition of communication is: A Sender > Transmits a Message (information) > Perceived by a Receiver. Writing is one form of communication; written communications are one form of information.

LESSON OBJECTIVE STATED

Librarian Script: "Today we're going to look at messages and identify the sender, the receiver, and what kinds of sources of information might contribute to crafting a credible message depending on the purpose of a written communication."

INPUT/MODELING

Before class, the librarian sets up the board with four columns. These will be for primary, secondary, and tertiary sources, and tools/containers; do not label them as such until later. The librarian writes the word *Information* on the board and poses questions to the class:

- What forms can information come in?
- Where are places you would find information?
- Can you use information to find more information?

Using a "Think (1 min), Pair (2 min), Share (5 min)" process,[2] the class generates lists on the board. Students call out any kinds of sources of information they can possibly suggest, while the librarian writes them on the board, making on-the-fly assignments to the source area columns.

Here are some prompts for the librarian to elicit types of sources from class:

- Format: oral, print, electronic
- Style: formal, informal
- Audience: scientists, students, Internet surfers

GUIDED PRACTICE

The librarian divides the class into small groups of three to four each and gives each group one of the following role sheets for taking notes.

- *High School Student.* You have an assignment to describe the relationship between smell and memory. Include and explain at least two scientific or technical terms or concepts.
- *Journalist.* You are researching a feature article for a news magazine or news web site about "DigiScent," a technology to develop "smell-enabled virtual reality."
- *Professor, Researcher, or Scholar.* You are a Psychology PhD with a special research expertise in memory and cognition. You are writing up the results of your most recent experimental study for publication.
- *College Student.* You have an assignment to write a personal reflection on a memory you have that you strongly associate with a particular smell or scent. Frame your reflection with

some supporting background information from technical, literary or artistic sources.

When gathering information, consider:
- who you are
- what your message is
- who your audience is

Using a broad topic, such as "smells that trigger memories," work in small groups to brainstorm a list of sources of information, depending on the considerations above.

The librarian circulates among the groups, listens in, and helps students focus. Call time after 10–12 minutes, and have each group share. As types of sources are mentioned, you can add an asterisk or circle them on the board. See how many of the ones on the board get mentioned by the groups.

SELF-ASSESSMENTS

The librarian refers back to the four columns on the board with sources filled in and leads discussion of the types of content in each column. The librarian prompts students to consider the following:
- Why are information items in columns? What do they have in common? (Elicit categories from class.)
- The librarian labels the columns, *primary, secondary, tertiary*, and *search tools*, noting that these categories depend on discipline and context.
- What makes something a "primary source"?
- Can something from columns two or three ever be a primary source? When?
- Note the difference in the content of column 4. These are containers of information and tools for searching.

At this point, the librarian can introduce the concept of the information life cycle, and how the information contained in the columns below fit within.

1	2	3	4
Lab Notebooks	Bibliographies	Handbooks	Library catalogs
Memos	Books	Dictionaries	Search engines
Personal or formal letters,	Review articles	Encyclopedias	Internet
emails	Commentaries	Databases	Google
Diaries	Biographies	Wikipedia	
Interviews		Textbooks	
Patents			
Scholarly journals articles			
Dissertations			
Theses			
First-hand information	**A step removed**	**Organized,**	**Containers for**
At or close to event	**An overview/**	**synthesized**	**information and**
	interpretation	(the other two	**tools for locating**
	of event	summed up)	**information items**
			or sources

NOTES

1. William F. Eadie, ed., *21st Century Communication: A Reference Handbook*, 2 vols., (Thousand Oaks, CA: SAGE Publications, Inc., 2009). doi: http://dx.doi.org/10.4135/9781412964005.
2. Frank Lyman, Jr., "The Development of Tools," *Maryland ATE Journal* 1 (1981): 20–21.

Starting Points: The Role of Blogs in Scholarly Conversation

Students examine blogs and blog posts and their role within the scholarly conversation. By asking and answering questions about blogs' attributes and content, students learn to consider the usefulness of blogs in their own research, informing them on scholarly topics and leading them to additional sources of scholarly information.

CONCEPT IN CONTEXT

The ongoing conversation that is scholarship encompasses a wide array of voices, taking place in various settings, from traditional academic writing to a plethora of online resources, including blogs, podcasts, and more. These resources are changing the way scholars are discovering information and engaging in discourse, and they are transforming the possibilities for students, in turn, to become participants in these conversations. Given the proliferation of informally- and self-published resources and their emerging role in scholarly conversations, becoming familiar with ways to use them can enhance the research process and help students understand the potential of blogs as research tools.

This lesson also potentially addresses the threshold concept of *Authority is Contextual and Constructed*. In blogs, unlike journal articles, the authority of the speaker is not established by a construct like peer review, and readers face the challenge of ascertaining through other means the credibility and authority of the speaker.

Blogs, as used in this lesson, also have the potential to illuminate for students the concept of *Searching as Strategic Exploration*. Accessing ideas through blogs can inspire readers to explore, seeking new information to answer questions that arise as part of the conversation.

Overlapping Threshold Concepts: This lesson also address the concepts of *Authority is Constructed and Contextual* and *Searching as Strategic Exploration*.

Author: Brandon West, Online Instruction/Instructional Design Librarian
State University of New York at Oswego

Level: Basic/general education
Estimated Time: 50 minutes

MATERIALS NEEDED
- A sample blog post (topic related to classroom context or assignment)
- A handout listing blog conversational attributes
- A handout listing discussion questions (*see Appendix or www. ala.org/acrl/files/handouts.pdf)*
- Computers or tablets with Internet access for student use

LEARNING GOALS
- Students will identify the role of blogs in scholarly conversation.
- Students will recognize the importance of evaluating the content of blogs as information for use in their own research.
- Students will use blogs to inspire and inform the search for additional information.

ANTICIPATORY SET
Librarian Script: "Imagine you walk up to a group of your friends in the cafeteria. They're engaged in a lively conversation; people are interrupting, disagreeing, nodding, and adding to the messy discussion. You're eager to hear what your friends have to say, and you want to be part of the conversation. What do you do to enter the conversation?"

The librarian leads discussion as a large group or asks students to break into small groups.

Note to the librarian: It's not necessary to spend too much time on this. The point of this anticipatory set is to liken a natural, social conversation to a scholarly conversation.

LESSON OBJECTIVE STATED
Librarian Script: "Today we are going to be looking at how blogs are used in the scholarly conversation and determine how to use blogs in your research."

INPUT/MODELING

Librarian Script:

Scholarship is a lot like a conversation. People have ideas based on evidence that they write and publish and then other people respond and add to those ideas. Sometimes there are disagreements and rebuttals, and sometimes new facts or ideas give rise to side conversations. These conversations are robust, lively and messy, and include a lot of voices.

(*Note to librarian:* The following points are ways in which scholarly and social conversations are similar. Elaborate these points as needed, and focus on the points that serve your students' purposes, depending on the assignment or research need.)

- You have to listen and observe before you contribute, in whatever form that may be.
- Both social and scholarly conversations involve different voices and viewpoints, backgrounds of knowledge, and some really great ideas. They also both involve some not-so-great ideas.
- In order to form solid contributions, you need to listen and evaluate the contributions of others.
- In both situations, if you offer a new viewpoint, you're expected to have some evidence to substantiate your claim.
- Both conversations can raise questions that inspire you to learn about something new with further research/follow-up. You may actually have more (hopefully better and more nuanced) questions than when you entered the conversation.

There are a lot of voices in any scholarly conversation. A blog is just one. Often assignment guidelines will dictate that you use scholarly sources such as journal articles as the basis of your research. Even though you may not end up using a blog in your final research paper, a blog can still be part of your research process. It might be used as a springboard to help you figure out a topic and help you generate ideas that inform your search for journal articles. It can help you enter the conversation or lead you to other voices within the conversation.

Blogs can be authored by anyone. While there can be value in a variety of opinions, it is important to start thinking about blogs from a scholarly perspective. Thinking critically about a blog can help you determine if the key ideas in the blog are worth exploring.

The librarian guides the students through a sample search to find a blog and they view it as a class. Together they consider a few main elements of the blog and how they relate to the idea of having a scholarly conversation:

- **Author:** Who wrote this blog? Why?
- Key idea(s) behind the blog post
- Comments: the responses represent a community of participants
- Further or related research: How might you go about finding more information about this topic?

GUIDED PRACTICE (PART 1)

The students will work in small groups to find (optional), review, and analyze a blog post. If time or technology is limited, the librarian will have blog post samples ready for students to view. Using the handout (*see Appendix or www.ala.org/acrl/files/handouts.pdf*), students consider the following attributes of a particular blog post.

Author: Name, Position/Occupation
Affiliated University/Organization

Purpose: Why did the author write this blog post?

Point of view: What are the author's biases? Does the author offer a balanced perspective?

Currency: Are the topics recent? Could the information be outdated?

References: Links or citations referring to other research, studies, or information

Comments: Responses, rebuttals, critiques, questions, or additional information from the blogging community

Names or Organizations: Individual researchers, experts, or other people mentioned

Facts or Data: Information facts for figures, linked or not linked

Blog Roll: What blogs does the blogger follow?

Related Research Ideas: Other topics mentioned in the blog/blog post

Keywords: Relevant ideas/phrases to use to search for more information

After students analyze the blog post, they will discuss their findings as a large group as facilitated by the librarian. This discussion reinforces the idea of scholarship as a conversation and leads to an opportunity to explore the concepts of authority and exploration as related to blogs.

GUIDED PRACTICE (PART 2)

Following the class discussion on the various attributes of the blog post, the librarian divides the class into three groups. Each group focuses on one set of questions as a way to view the blog attributes through the lens of authority, strategic exploration, or scholarly conversation. The small group conversations can be followed by a class discussion in which the groups present their findings. Alternatively, depending on time, level, and need, the librarian can choose to focus on and/or facilitate just one of these discussions.

CHECK FOR UNDERSTANDING

While the students work in their groups, the librarian should be walking around the room and listening to student conversations. Doing so will allow the librarian to address questions and observe student behavior.

During or after the group discussion, the librarian asks the following questions:

- How might you use blogs in your research?
- How do blogs contribute to scholarly conversations?

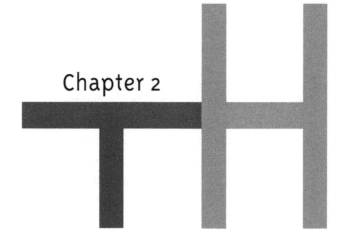

Chapter 2

Research as Inquiry

MANY NEW COLLEGE students view research as limited to the investigative process carried out by scientists and scholars. They do not see themselves as researchers even though they, too, discover facts new to them and must analyze the information they find. To become confident researchers, students need to first understand the collaborative, conversational nature of scholarship to recognize not only their role in it, but also find a path to enter it. *Research as Inquiry* describes the process by which researchers ask questions or state problems in order to find answers to contribute to the larger body of existing research within a discipline. This idea is sometimes referred to as "finding gaps in the knowledge." Gap-finding, however, may prove difficult for students who are not already familiar with the existing literature or body of knowledge.

This threshold concept is, in a sense, the stepping-off point for many students to find, understand, and use information. The process of formulating a research question or identifying a problem is a self-directed one. It requires a willingness to be open to new ideas, new or differing points of view, and a level of uncertainty that may feel, to a novice, unsettling. Moreover, such investigation is rooted within a discipline that may be new to the student as well. The librarian can ease students' discomfort and unfamiliarity by using lessons that instill confidence and curiosity and demonstrate that research is a reiterative process that begins by building on an initial question or idea. It is the process through which students and scholars develop a deeper understanding of a discipline. The activities in these lessons encourage students to view their research through the lens of inquiry and to approach the information-seeking process fully aware that questions may not lead to answers but instead to more questions. This openness of thought and direction helps students get a clear picture of the scholarly conversation around a topic and formulate a more precise question for their own research within that conversation.

To find useful information, one must know what to look for and where to look. Charissa Jefferson's lesson about the research discussion starts here. It gets students thinking about the purpose of research and about how the work they do is part of a larger picture. When students see their research role and understand the purpose behind the investigation, they can better focus their ideas and their questions. A focused information search requires a discipline-specific language. When students learn where and how their work fits into the research process, they can better understand the importance of effective search language for worthwhile results. The lesson by Kevin Klipfel models the process of articulating the question, using a narrative approach. By laying bare the process by which a researcher comes up with the problem statement, research question, or hypothesis, Klipfel's activities get inside the head of a researcher so as to help students better understand how to develop an idea worth investigating.

Sarah Naumann and Sami Lange consider the affective domain by having students examine their personal information-seeking behavior to highlight the similarities between personal and academic information and break down inhibitions on the part of novice researchers. Information seeking in one's personal life is fueled by inquiry and the desire to know; this same spirit of inquiry should be underlying academic research. Students begin to recognize that we are all continually seeking information for countless purposes. Academic research is one of those purposes, with learnable structures and methods.

Robert Farrell's and Smita Avasthi's approaches to this concept are somewhat unusual. Farrell likens research to a crime scene investigation, focusing on the iterative nature of the process. Rather than focusing on the answers one discovers via the inquiry process, this lesson emphasizes the idea that new knowledge can lead to new questions. Students practice asking increasingly complex questions based on information they find, much like the process followed by a detective. Avasthi's lesson on flawed research questions encourages students to look critically at the question to see its potential flaws, such as over-specificity or irrelevance, to craft the optimal course for their research.

The lessons in this chapter enter the research process at its various stages. They use natural language, encouraging students to equate the research they do in their course work to the question-and-answer processes they use in their everyday lives. The lessons teach students to recognize research strategies such as: *motivation, discussion, narration, satisfying curiosity,* and *thinking-through.* By reflecting on their own personal strategies for answering questions or solving problems, students can compare their processes to those in an academic setting and apply those same critical thinking skills to their academic research.

Flawed Questions: Tools for Inquiry

This exercise asks students to identify problems in a series of research questions and to rewrite the questions so they are suitable for essay topics.

CONCEPT IN CONTEXT

Inquiry is a process "that focuses on problems or questions in a discipline or between disciplines that are open or unresolved."[1] We seek information to answer questions or explain issues and problems. To find the best answer; i.e., the most appropriate information, we must ask the right questions. Sometimes researchers arrive at the right questions by asking the wrong questions first and then refining them. This iterative process requires curiosity and willingness to make mistakes and learn from those mistakes.

Many times students develop questions that are either too broad or too narrow, or they may phrase their questions in a way that does not lend them to argument or analysis, such as asking a yes-or-no question. In this lesson, the librarian can lead students to use flawed questions as part of the research process.

Author: Dr. Smita Avasthi, Public Services and Lead Instruction Librarian
Santa Rosa Junior College, Santa Rosa, California

Level: Basic
Estimated Time: 50–60 minutes

MATERIALS NEEDED

- An optional handout for students containing examples of flawed research questions (*see Appendix or www.ala.org/acrl/files/handouts.pdf*)

LEARNING GOALS

- By evaluating and revising flawed research questions, students will learn strategies to formulate appropriate research questions for lower-division undergraduate essays.

- Students will apply what they have learned to their own research questions.

ANTICIPATORY SET

Librarian Script: "Instructors often give you the opportunity to choose your own subject to research and write about. This gives you the freedom to explore what interests you the most. But it can sometimes be very hard to come up with a good research question. A research question is a way of approaching a problem or issue to study. For example, you may want to write about capital punishment. But what specifically do you want to know about capital punishment? There are many issues associated with capital punishment and you will be quickly overwhelmed with information. You must clarify your research by framing your topic in the form of a focused question that allows for investigation. For example, a more focused and manageable research question about the issue of capital punishment might be: 'Is capital punishment a deterrent to murder?'"

LESSON OBJECTIVE STATED

Librarian Script: "In today's lesson we will look at some research questions and work together to determine if they are appropriate questions for a research assignment. If we decide they are not, we will discuss ways to refine them. You will then be able to spend time evaluating and refining your own research question."

INPUT/MODELING

The librarian will first lead the students in a whole class exercise. The librarian will write a research question on the board and/or refer students to one on their handout, for example, "How has the Internet changed our lives?"

The librarian will engage students in a discussion about that question. For example, s/he can ask students if they think it is a good research question. If students answer yes, they are asked to defend that answer. If no, the librarian asks for ideas about how to make it a more appropriate research question. The librarian can lead the class by modeling techniques to revise the question until the class agrees that the question is more suitable for a research project. For example, the original question might be too broad, so the demonstration would focus on how to narrow that question by setting it in context or specifying a time or demographic group.

This particular example question, "How has the Internet changed our lives?" is too broad and unfocused. Whose lives have been changed? Has it changed the lives of young people more than the lives of older people? What particular aspects of our lives does the Internet effect? A more appropriate and manageable topic might be "How has the Internet affected the way college students write research papers?"

GUIDED PRACTICE

Once the librarian has led the students through the process, the students should be divided into pairs or small groups. Each pair/group will be assigned one of the flawed research questions on the handout. The librarian instructs students to evaluate their assigned question and rewrite it based on the techniques they have learned and with reference to the prompts on their handout.

The students are given time to brainstorm with each other to rewrite the questions in any way that they choose, as long as they do not alter the general topic or discipline.

Each student group is asked to report their revised research questions, which are then discussed by the class as a whole. During this process, the librarian highlights how the group has revised the question and asks for further refinement, particularly if the question is still unmanageable. The librarian guides the discussion until the question becomes more suitable.

SELF-ASSESSMENT

Students can then be directed to analyze their own research questions. They can be prompted to explain how or why their question no longer has the problems they identified earlier and why their question is suitable for their class assignment. These explanations can be used to assess whether students can apply their skills.

NOTES

1.   Information Literacy Competency Standards for Higher Education Task Force, *Framework for Information Literacy for Higher Education,* Draft 1, Part 1. (Chicago: Association of College and Research Libraries, February, 2014, 13). http://acrl.ala.org/ilstandards/wp-content/uploads/2014/02/Framework-for-IL-for-HE-Draft-1-Part-1.pdf.

Crime Scene Investigation as an Analogy for Scholarly Inquiry

By comparing the steps of researching and writing a paper to the steps taken by crime scene investigators, students learn that research is an iterative process through which new knowledge leads to new questions.

CONCEPT IN CONTEXT

Lower-level college students are usually mystified by the scholarly research process. Most undergraduates come to college with little or no formal research instruction and have seen no practical examples of real-world scholarly inquiry or output. This lesson provides students with a practical analogy for scholarly inquiry using an example they are all familiar with, crime scene investigation. By comparing the steps taken in researching and writing a paper to those taken by investigators as they examine a crime scene, the librarian helps students understand that research "is iterative and depends upon asking increasingly complex or new questions whose answers in turn develop additional questions or lines of inquiry in any field."[1]

Author: Robert Farrell, Assistant Professor, Library Coordinator of Information Literacy and Assessment
Lehman College, City University of New York

Level: Basic

Estimated Time: 30 minutes

This lesson can work as a whole class activity/discussion or students can be divided into teams. The goal is for students to arrive at independently derived structures of the inquiry process that can then be brought back to the larger group for discussion.

MATERIALS NEEDED

- White board, chalk board, or smart board

LEARNING GOALS

- Students will become familiar with the inquiry process.

- Students will recognize scholarship as the independent production of new knowledge.
- Students will appreciate the role of inquiry as a habit essential to all independent learning.

ANTICIPATORY SET

The librarian begins class with a discussion of the following questions:

- How many of you have ever written a research paper before?
- Why have you been asked to write a research paper for this course?
- Will you be asked to write research papers again after this course?
- Why are you asked to write research papers not just once, but many times?

LESSON OBJECTIVE STATED

Librarian Script: "Today we will try to answer the question of why we are asked to write research papers in college, not just once but many times. We want to be able to say what the ultimate point of our work is. To do so, we will define research as a process of inquiry and compare it to a form of inquiry we are all familiar with. Based on this analogy, we will try to understand what we can accomplish not just in college, but in everyday life if we are able to successfully undertake inquiries for ourselves."

INPUT/MODELING

The librarian asks students, "What does the word 'inquiry' mean? What does it mean to inquire?" The idea of questioning/asking questions is thus educed.

The librarian divides a whiteboard into two columns. On one side the librarian writes "CSI" and asks students if they know what the acronym means. Crime scene investigation is a popular topic in popular culture and forensics a growing field. A clip from the beginning of an episode of *CSI* or similar show or movie can be shown (optional). The librarian poses the next question: "What do crime scene investigators do?"

By working through a number of questions posed by the librarian, students articulate the following series of steps (or something like them) that comprise an inquiry into a crime scene.

Crime Scene Investigation = Inquiry

1. Get big picture of the crime scene (circle with yellow tape)
2. Analyze crime scene—break into parts (evidence, witnesses)
3. Ask questions (of witnesses, of evidence in lab)
4. Answer questions (which may raise new questions; repeat 3 & 4 as needed; this step gets at the iterative nature of inquiry)
5. Synthesize answers—solve crime
6. Present argument in court that organizes answers to questions

Questions the librarian can pose:

- What does a crime scene investigator do first when they get to a crime scene?
- After delimiting the crime scene (determining the big picture that needs to be investigated) what is their next step?
- Once the crime scene is analyzed into what's important and what's not, what must the crime scene investigator do with the evidence/witnesses?

Having completed the first step of the inquiry process, the class turns to the other half of the whiteboard and compares crime scene investigation to writing research papers, again through discussion. Based on the first discussion some variation of the following typically results:

Research Paper = Inquiry

1. Get big picture of a topic
2. Analyze topic—break into parts (subtopics, related issues)
3. Ask questions
4. Answer questions—using information sources (which again may raise new questions; repeat 3 & 4 as needed; this step gets at the "iterative" nature of inquiry)
5. Synthesize answers—thinking about information
6. Present argument in paper that organizes answers to questions

Having clearly established the process common to both forms of inquiry, the class reconsiders the answers given to the question of why students write research papers. The earlier answers are correlated to the steps in the processes outlined. The librarian can typically point out that none of the earlier answers takes into account the whole process that has been laid out.

The question is posed again: "Why do you write research papers in college—not once, but many times?"

Turning to the crime scene investigation column, the librarian begins a new inquiry, asking:

1.   How much does the investigator know when the case starts?
2.   How much does the investigator know at the end?
3.   What did the investigator do from start to finish?
4.   Who made and presented the discovery?

By answering these questions, students begin to see an analogy. Students discover that just as crime scene investigators independently learn who committed a crime and are responsible for that discovery and its cogent articulation, so too do students start out knowing little about a topic and know more by the end. Further, they, like investigators, must "make a case" and articulate what they have learned. Inquiry is established as a method of independent learning. When writing research papers, students engage in inquiries through which they learn to build on what they discover and become producers of new knowledge, i.e., scholars.

The answer the class started with is posed for the final time: "Why do you write research papers in college—not once, but many times?" with the focus on "but many times."

The librarian asks, "What happens when you do something over and over again?"

The librarian directs the discussion toward the idea that through writing multiple research papers students acquire habits of independent learning and argument building. These habits are characteristic of scholars and others who must learn and demonstrate their learning.

GUIDED PRACTICE

The remainder of class session is given over to a group inquiry into a topic using the library's resources. This models the steps of the inquiry process uncovered through the previous discussion.

CHECK FOR UNDERSTANDING

By its nature, the Socratic Method checks for learning as the inquiry into the nature of inquiry progresses. The librarian can ask students to recognize analogies between the one set up in the lesson and other everyday activities/phenomena.

INDEPENDENT PRACTICE

Disciplinary faculty can assign their students a short, metacognitive writing assignment as an appendix to their final research papers by asking them to reflect on and articulate the steps of the inquiry process they undertook to complete their papers.

ACKNOWLEDGMENTS

The author would like to acknowledge his colleagues for their continued discussion of and participation in the development of this exercise, particularly Jennifer King, who floated the notion of CSI in an early instructional meeting, and Stefanie Havelka for introducing video clips into her sessions.

NOTES

1.   Information Literacy Competency Standards for Higher Education Task Force. "Framework for Information Literacy for Higher Education, Final Draft." Chicago: Association of College and Research Libraries, January 16, 2015. http://acrl.ala.org/ilstandards/wp-content/uploads/2015/01/Framework-MW15-Board-Docs.pdf.

The Research Discussion

This lesson prompts students to think about the motivation behind research and asks them to do research at a very basic level.

CONCEPT IN CONTEXT

While college students understand that their education requires them to do research, they do not always understand the purpose of that research, beyond achieving an acceptable grade. When librarians enable students to see research as a process that incorporates disagreement and requires reiteration, students can then take part in it. Research done in the context of a specific course has little meaning outside of the classroom. Students who understand that the work they do is part of a larger, integrated process where new knowledge is added to existing knowledge begin to make sense of their role within it. By completing this exercise, students begin to realize that research serves to ask and answer questions and add new knowledge to existing knowledge, thus allowing them to join in the scholarly conversation.

> **Author**:   Charissa Jefferson, Business and Data Librarian
> *California State University, Northridge*
>
> **Level:**   Basic/general education
> **Estimated Time**: 30–45 minutes

MATERIALS NEEDED

- Computers with Internet access

LEARNING GOALS

- Students will understand the foundational purpose of conducting research.
- Students will recognize that researchers gather information to answer questions, to integrate into their own work, and to create new information.

ANTICIPATORY SET

To get the students to begin thinking about the lesson, the librarian can pose these questions to the class: "A college education requires doing research.

But what is research? Why do we do research? What are the benefits? What does it mean to do research?"

Ideally, the conversation will lead to the notion that research is gathering data and analyzing information to answer a question.

LESSON OBJECTIVE STATED

Librarian Script: "Today we are going to look at a question and determine how to answer that question with only the knowledge we have, based on our experience. Then we will attempt to answer that same question by seeking information that will help us answer the question using various information resources."

INPUT/MODELING

The librarian asks a general question about which the answer can be assumed based on experience and/or personal knowledge. Example: "In what ways does lack of sleep affect student performance?"

The students write their answers without having done any research. The librarian leads a short discussion that solicits students' answers, their sources of information, and their assessment of the reliability of the answers. Students should begin to recognize the need for reliable information.

Next, students independently research the topic using Google and/or library research tools to attempt to answer the question. The librarian then demonstrates a search in which students examine the variety of search results for their varying perspectives and data.

The librarian discusses with the class how the evidence found in the research supports (or refutes) the initial students' answers to the question. The librarian points out the connections among results, the various directions taken by researchers, and the different questions asked and answered.

CHECK FOR UNDERSTANDING

The following questions can be used in a class discussion to gauge student understanding and reinforce the conceptual underpinnings of the lesson.
- What are the benefits of the research?
- How are these articles related to one another?
- If we liken the research to a conversation on sleep deprivation, what do the different researchers have say about it?

Developing a Research Question: Topic Selection

The librarian uses an authentic language narrative to model the "thinking-through" process of research. The narrative encourages students to consider the widest possible range of ideas when embarking on a research assignment. The lesson shows students that research is a process of inquiry that can be driven as much by individual interest as by professorial assignment.

CONCEPT IN CONTEXT

New college students may struggle with the seemingly straightforward idea that research is a process of inquiry. Some will hear from their professors the directive to "look for gaps in the literature" in order to formulate a topic worthy of research. How does one identify such gaps without a healthy familiarity with the literature? A student without research experience learns by first observing a model, then practicing. In this lesson, students see and hear the librarian think through the preliminary stages of the research process and gain insight into its iterative nature. The librarian begins with an idea, asks an initial question, and follows it with related, more involved questions. The narrative approach used here aims to make students comfortable with the process and encourages students to propose, within the parameters of their disciplinary assignment, a research question that interests them, not one that merely fulfills a requirement. Students learn in this activity that the subjects and ideas that excite them personally can inspire and motivate them academically. When students choose a topic in which they already have interest and/or experience, the pathway to finding the gaps is smoothed and they can focus on the process of questioning, reflecting, and repeating.

Author: Kevin Michael Klipfel, Information Literacy Coordinator
California State University, Chico

Level: Basic/General Education
Estimated Time: 50–60 minutes

MATERIALS NEEDED

- Keyword exercise worksheet (*See Appendix or www.ala.org/acrl/ files/handouts.pdf*)

LEARNING GOALS

- Students will learn to turn a personal interest into a question or questions for further investigation.
- Students will learn to focus a research question (or set of related questions) from their preliminary investigation, based on information available to them through library resources and/or the Web.
- Students will learn that research and learning are inspired by authentic interest and intellectual curiosity.
- Students will learn to identify keywords on a topic to use in the search for information.

ANTICIPATORY SET

At this stage in the research process, students should have begun to think about possible topics they might research for their assignment. Asking students what they are thinking of working on and why it interests them can initiate a dialogue about topic selection and the reasons students have chosen particular topics. This exercise is a good icebreaker and serves as a useful transition to introduce the main learning objectives of the session.

The librarian might ask the students how many times they have found themselves bored with a topic they were working on and what makes a paper more interesting to work on.

LESSON OBJECTIVE STATED

Librarian Script:

> What we're going to learn today is how to develop a research question and to use the library to search for information on that question. We'll use your specific assignment as an example. Almost every paper you write in college requires you to choose a topic and develop a research question, so it's a very useful skill to learn.

The best way to choose a topic is to write about something you are passionate about. I'm going to show you how to take an authentic personal interest—something that you care about and that's meaningful to you—and develop a researchable topic from that interest, even within the parameters of your class assignment. This will be a valuable skill throughout the rest of your college career. It will help you be more invested in your schoolwork and use your educational experience to explore things that matter to you.

INPUT/MODELING

The librarian models how to choose a topic and search for information by demonstrating an *authentic narrative*: walking students, verbally and visually, step-by-step through the process of how the librarian chose a topic that authentically interested her or him(based on the requirements of the assignment). The goal is to show the students *how* to approach the research process, not just tell them they should do so.

The librarian gives the class a research topic as an example. This sample topic about student health is provided:

Research a recent finding, published in the last five years, relating to student health, and write a three-to-five-page essay discussing the findings. Make a recommendation to the University Health Center about a way to improve student services. Use only scholarly sources as evidence to support your statements.

The librarian then speaks to the class, modeling the thinking process of embarking on a research project. The "speech" will reflect the initial confusion, the stream-of-consciousness of ideas that precede actual keyword identification (sample narrative):

Looking at this assignment, I'm not quite sure how to fit my interests within the scope of this topic. What, if anything, can I write about regarding student health that interests me? I'm interested in meditation because, I guess; it's supposed to be a way to reduce stress. Maybe, within the context of this assignment, I could write about whether or not meditation reduces stress. I wonder if there's any research on that.

So, there's my tentative topic: Does meditation reduce stress? Maybe I could even focus on college students. So then, my topic could be: Can meditation reduce stress among college students? That might work, because I'm interested in meditation and reducing stress through meditation would fit with this assignment. If the research does show that meditation reduces stress, I could recommend to the Health Center that they offer meditation instruction to students, since lots of students deal with stress, especially during final exams.

GUIDED PRACTICE

The librarian demonstrates the keyword exercise. As in the Input/Modeling, the librarian talks the students through the process of finding the major ideas within the topic and identifying the keywords or search words for beginning a database search (sample narrative):

Now we have our tentative topic/question: does meditation reduce stress in college students? Now, I need to search for information on my topic. How do I go about doing that?

The first thing I want to do is pull out the major research ideas. I can do this by taking my tentative topic [librarian writes topic on board] and underline the main ideas: meditation, reducing stress, college students. These are my major "keywords" or search words I'll use to search the library or the Internet.

I might have to do several searches and I might have to create different word combinations, but I can start with just one word, like meditation. I can try different variations on the words, too, like reducing stress or stress reduction. Searching is a process; there probably won't be one source that will answer all my questions.

The students are then given approximately five minutes to fill out the keyword exercise worksheet. The librarian can ask one or two students to share their process so that other students may benefit from seeing how their peers completed the exercise. The librarian can then model for students how to search for library resources on an authentic question of interest.

See section on Searching as Strategic Exploration for lesson ideas.

INDEPENDENT PRACTICE

The majority of the session is then devoted to deliberative practice of these information literacy skills. Students will work independently to further refine their topics and search for information with their keywords using library resources. The librarian will walk around the classroom to talk with students, provide individual feedback about searches, and assist students.

The Connection between Personal and Academic Research

This multi-session lesson asks students to examine their personal informa-tion-seeking behavior and compare it to academic research. When they real-ize academic research is similar to what they do every day they usually feel more inspired and confident in their research.

CONCEPT IN CONTEXT

Many students are not confident in their ability to find appropriate infor-mation for their research papers. They do not realize that searching for information on a research topic is similar to what they do every day when they look up information about a new gym or restaurant or search for infor-mation about traveling to Cancún for spring break. It is the question or the problem that prompts the search. By drawing this real-world connection to academic information seeking, this lesson demonstrates to students that the process of inquiry is something they have already performed and, at some level, already understand. From this basic understanding, students can begin to search for and deal with new questions, opposing viewpoints, and views through other disciplinary lenses. When students are able to view research as a means to satisfy their academic curiosity rather than ful-fill an obligation, they can take genuine interest in the process. This lesson is a first step in developing an understanding that, in academic research, there may be more than one answer or no answer at all. We cannot, how-ever, find a good answer without first asking a good question.

Authors: Sarah Naumann, Literacy Program Coordinator
*San Mateo Public Library, San Mateo, California;
Adjunct Faculty, Library Instruction, California State
University, East Bay*

Sami Lange, Public Services and Instruction Librarian
Santa Rosa Junior College, Santa Rosa, California

Level: Basic—suitable for freshman with little experience in online searching

Estimated Time: This three-part assignment was originally designed to be part of a semester- long information literacy course. It can easily be adapted for a face-to-face class or parts can be used in a single session. At full length, each session is 50–60 minutes.

MATERIALS NEEDED

- If the lesson is taught as a part of an online course, students should have access to a discussion board where they can see each other's work. No handouts or supplemental materials are needed.

LEARNING GOAL

- Students will learn that the process of searching for personal information is very similar to the process of academic research.

PART I

A discussion board assignment called "Ten Questions" is given to the students early in a semester-long introduction to information literacy course, e.g. week two of a 10-week course. It is an attention grabber that engages students in the course and allows them to get to know their peers.

ANTICIPATORY SET

Librarian Script:

> Although you probably don't think about it, you search for and use information every day. For example:
>
> - You search for and purchase a book from Amazon.com.
> - You check out the hours of a restaurant to make sure they are open before you go.
> - You search for a video on YouTube.
> - You look for articles for a paper you are writing in class.
>
> Your first assignment in this class is for you to spend some time thinking about your information needs.

INPUT/MODELING

Introduction of Discussion Board Assignment: "Ten Questions"
Librarian Script:

Your discussion board assignment this week requires you to take a three-hour time period and write down all of your information needs. Pick a time that involves you doing a lot of things. Examples include working, hanging out with friends, doing homework or going to an internship. Do not pick a time when you will be completely involved in something that does not require much thinking or questioning, such as while you are watching a movie or playing a video game.

Your task for the board is to write down every (yes, every) question you had during that three-hour period. We are always seeking information. After you write down your questions, go back and write down what type of information you needed in the following categories.

Personal—relating to your private life

Academic—course-related assignments

Professional—relating to your job or internship

Statistical—looking for data

You should have a minimum of ten questions in your three-hour period; the more the better, because we will be evaluating these questions in upcoming weeks.

Examples
- What art schools on the west coast offer graduate programs?
  Type of information need: Personal
- How late is the bakery near my home open?
  Type of information need: Personal

- My paper is due tomorrow. Where can I find five peer-reviewed sources.
  Type of information need: Academic

After you have posted your own questions, comment on two of your classmates' posts by replying to their posts. In your reply answer this question:

Do you think your classmate identified the correct type of information need? If not, identify the type of information need you think they have.

PART II

Week following introduction of assignment

INPUT/MODELING

The librarian discusses the importance of analyzing questions which can include the following:

Librarian Script: "A great deal of our time is spent asking questions, whether these are formally stated or thoughts we have. By identifying the question and type of information need, you are taking steps toward searching and researching."

The librarian introduces the next assignment.

Librarian Script:

Referring back to the ten questions you wrote for the first assignment in this class, I want you to analyze each of them with respect to the following four questions, paying special attention to questions 3 and 4.

1. What is my question?

2. What *type* of questions is it/ what *type* of information need is it? (Personal, academic, professional or statistical?)

3. Where will I look for answers to this question?

4. How will I search for this question? What type of search strategy will I use?

If your question type is personal, but it involves needing information about local restaurants, how will you search for this and where? In Google, Yelp, Urbanspoon?

If your question is academic, e.g. for a research paper or assignment, you will most likely need to use acceptable scholarly sources. Often this means using books, scholarly journals, and online library databases that can be accessed through your library website.

CHECK FOR UNDERSTANDING

- Students analyze the work of their peers.
- Students learn to identify their information needs.
- Students comment on their findings in the weekly reflections.

PART III

Part three of the "Ten Questions" assignment is given later in semester, e.g., in week eight of a ten-week class. It involves applying what students have learned about searching and analyzing information. At this stage in the semester, students should have:

1. Learned simple and advanced search techniques
2. Learned to use the library databases and advanced searching in Google
3. Learned to use the library catalog
4. Analyzed websites and identified appropriate academic sources

LESSON OBJECTIVE STATED

Librarian Script: "The purpose of this part of your assignment is to use your new search skills to answer your own questions from week two. The idea is that all questions, whether personal, or for academic research, can be addressed in the same way."

INPUT/MODELING

Librarian Script: "We are going to revisit the ten questions assignment you did for week two. Choose three of your questions. One question must be academic, one personal, and one professional. Then, using your new search skills, look for the answer to your questions.

"Remember, searching is a process. The more you practice, the better you will get. If you do not find the perfect source, what other sources did you find that may help you get there?"

GUIDED PRACTICE

Practicing newly-acquired research skills with their own questions allows students to see the connection between personal questions and academic questions. Students are not afraid to answer their own questions and this confidence helps them to move on to answering academic questions. Students generally make the connection between researching their own questions and academic questions. If students struggle with this, the librarian can comment on their work and make suggestions for further study.

INDEPENDENT PRACTICE

At this point in the semester, students go back to researching their chosen topic. Most students understand the concepts of the exercise and are able to move forward with their research with a greater understanding of analyzing a question and researching it.

This threshold concept is, in a sense, the stepping-off point for many students to find, understand, and use information. The process of formulating a research question or identifying a problem is a self-directed one. It requires a willingness to be open to new ideas, new or differing points of view, and a level of uncertainty that may feel, to a novice, unsettling. Moreover, such investigation is rooted within a discipline that may be new to the student as well. The librarian can ease students' discomfort and unfamiliarity by using lessons that instill confidence and curiosity and demonstrate that research is a reiterative process that begins by building on an initial question or idea. It is the process through which students and scholars develop a deeper understanding of a discipline. The activities in these lessons encourage students to view their research through the lens of inquiry and to approach the information-seeking process fully aware that questions may not lead to answers but instead to more questions. This openness of thought and direction helps students get a clear picture of the scholarly conversation around a topic and formulate a more precise question for their own research within that conversation.

To find useful information, one must know what to look for and where to look. Charissa Jefferson's lesson about the research discussion starts here. It gets students thinking about the purpose of research and about how the work they do is part of a larger picture. When students see their research role and understand the purpose behind the investigation, they can better focus their ideas and their questions. A focused information search requires a discipline-specific language. When students learn where and how their work fits into the research process, they can better understand the importance of effective search language for worthwhile results. The lesson by Kevin Klipfel models the process of articulating the question, using a narrative approach. By laying bare the process by which a researcher comes up with the problem statement, research question, or hypothesis, Klipfel's activities get inside the head of a researcher so as to help students better understand how to develop an idea worth investigating.

Sarah Naumann considers the affective domain by having students examine their personal information-seeking behavior to highlight the similarities between personal and academic information and break down inhibitions on the part of novice researchers. Information seeking in one's personal life is fueled by inquiry and the desire to know; this same spirit of inquiry should be underlying academic research. Students begin to recognize that we are all continually seeking information for countless purposes. Academic research is one of those purposes, with learnable structures and methods.

Robert Farrell's and Smita Avasthi's approaches to this concept are somewhat unusual. Farrell likens research to a crime scene investigation, focusing on the iterative nature of the process. Rather than focusing on the answers one discovers via the inquiry process, this lesson emphasizes the idea that new knowledge can lead to new questions. Students practice asking increasingly complex questions based on information they find, much like the process followed by a detective. Avasthi's lesson on flawed research questions encourages students to look critically at the question to see its potential flaws, such as over-specificity or irrelevance, to craft the optimal course for their research.

The lessons in this chapter enter the research process at its various stages. They use natural language, encouraging students to equate the research they do in their course work to the question-and-answer processes they use in their everyday lives. The lessons teach students to recognize research strategies such as: motivation, discussion, narration, satisfying curiosity, and thinking-through. By reflecting on their own personal strategies for answering questions or solving problems, students can compare their processes to those in an academic setting and apply those same critical thinking skills to their academic research.

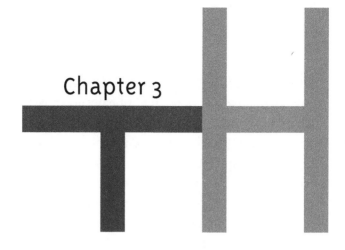

Chapter 3

Authority is Constructed and Contextual

THE AUTHORITY OF information, or the influence it carries with users, is entirely dependent on the context in which it is used and by whom. Authority is not synonymous with expertise and expertise does not guarantee authority. Authority may be the result of exposure, popularity disciplinary familiarity, or prestige. The leading authority on a subject is not necessarily an expert on that subject. Novice researchers, by necessity, may rely on the advice of instructors or, in some circumstances, find themselves restricted by prescriptive requirements for information sources. In spite of this fact, or perhaps because of it, it is imperative that students understand how authority may be constructed and why some information comes to be regarded as more trustworthy or valuable than others. As students begin to understand that their need for information and the purpose for which they will use it determines the value of that information, they can be more proficient seekers of information and more competent users of what they find.

The lessons in this chapter deal with the notions of authority and expertise within the context of use and discipline in a variety of ways. The idea that one's expertise on a subject does not always translate into authority on that subject is discussed in a lesson by Steven Hoover. His lesson gets students to create their own evaluative criteria for assessing the information they find outside of the traditionally accepted descriptive markers of "peer review" or "scholarly." Such terms refer to value indicators that students and faculty have learned to accept and trust, often without consideration of the construct that defines them. This lesson helps demonstrate to students that "peer review" is a process and that "scholarly" is an adjective, not an infallible category. In showing students that quality information can be found in unlikely places as long as one understands its purpose and examines it critically, librarians prepare them to be discerning users of information in the classroom and beyond.

Robert Farrell approaches the concept of authority from the perspective of the student in his lesson on evaluating information sources. He asks students to consider their own areas of expertise and how that specialized knowledge affects their interpretation of authority on that subject. By considering how they determine who is an authority on a topic in which they believe themselves to be very knowledgeable, they can appreciate the same process in a scholarly context. They begin to see how and, more importantly, *why* context matters. They can realize that authority is created, not endowed.

In a lesson that examines the use of news releases and blog posts as research information sources, Rachel Minkin focuses on disciplinary discourse. Her lesson teaches students to use non-scholarly information sources as research tools that build familiarity with the language and culture of a specific discipline. Recognizing trusted sources of information in a discipline requires understanding the issues within that discipline and the principal modes of communication among its researchers and interested participants. Scholars and experienced researchers know this and are able to recognize useful information from a variety of sources. Students unfamiliar to the discourse of a particular discipline are less able to discern good information from all that is available to them.

Lessons by Nancy Fawley and Jo Angela Oehrli and Emily Hamstra reiterate the importance of context and help students reflect on their need and use for the information they seek. Fawley's lesson gives students real-life examples of information in order to create a list of considerations when determining the value of information. Oehrli and Hamstra ask students to consider the information creators. As in all of the lessons in this chapter, they emphasize the context of use in determining the authority of the creator and the appropriateness of the information.

Evaluating Information Sources

Students reflect on their own expertise in a particular area in order to understand their implicit information evaluation processes. Making these explicit allows them to improve information evaluation in other areas in which they are less knowledgeable.

CONCEPT IN CONTEXT

This threshold concept is likely to be troublesome to students until they can appreciate that they, too, are authorities on a subject. On the surface, this lesson seems simple; it asks students to evaluate what they know and how they know it. It can be effective in its subtlety, however. By having students evaluate their own authority on a particular subject, this lesson breaks down troublesome knowledge about the evaluation of authority. Students begin to understand how authority is bestowed and how it is determined by context. Our everyday information seeking behavior is not vastly different from a researcher's information-seeking behavior. A student looking to repair a bicycle knows the process s/he follows to consult the proper source or person for the task. Asking students to compare this same critical analysis to their scholarly work empowers them to be skeptical researchers and to seek out more than superficial, handy bits of information.

> **Author:**   Robert Farrell, Assistant Professor, Library Coordinator
> of Information Literacy and Assessment
> *Lehman College, City University of New York*

Level: Basic
Estimated Time: 45 minutes

MATERIALS NEEDED
- Students need pens/pencils and paper
- White board, chalk board, or smart board
- Handout *(see Appendix or www.ala.org/acrl/files/handouts.pdf for handout)*

LEARNING GOALS

- Students will discover the different ways novices and experts evaluate information by reflecting on their own everyday information-seeking behaviors.
- Students will develop and apply a checklist for evaluating information.
- Students will actively attempt to corroborate a claim made in an information source.

ANTICIPATORY SET

Librarian Script: "Everyone in this room is an expert at something, even if it's something as simple as making toast."

LESSON OBJECTIVE STATED

Librarian Script: "You will think about the information evaluation processes you use in areas in which you are an expert. You will consider how those processes are similar to or different from those you use when you don't know a lot about something."

INPUT/MODELING

Students are asked to define the following terms in their own words:

1. Critical Thinking
2. Evaluation
3. Expert
4. Expertise

Students then share their thoughts, and the librarian records them on the board. Definitions of the terms are built out of students' preexisting understanding, with supplementation from a dictionary if needed.

The librarian groups students in pairs and displays or distributes the following questions:

- What are you an expert at?
- What did you have to do to acquire that expertise?

- If you meet someone who claims to be expert in the same thing you are, how do you know that s/he really is? How do you evaluate her or him?
- What is the difference between what you do to evaluate something in your area of expertise and what you do when you're not an expert?

The librarian explains that each pair of students should interview one another and record each other's answers. (Note: Instruction should specify the order of the interview—the person with the shorter hair first interviewing the person with the longer hair; the taller person first interviewing the shorter person; etc., in order to expedite the interviews.)

Once students have finished interviewing each other, the librarian reconvenes the class as a whole and has each pair report back. The librarian records in brief the answers provided, drawing parallels between answers as they arise. Through the discussion, students begin to make explicit the tacit processes they intuitively engage in when evaluating whether the people they meet or things they see or read are, in fact, reliable sources of information.

GUIDED PRACTICE

Students can be given any number of brief exercises designed to lead them through the steps of evaluating and corroborating informative readings or sources of information: a blog post about music from a random fan vs. a review from a national newspaper or magazine; an excerpt from a documentary vs. a publicly posted video on the same topic; competing op-ed articles on a topic; and so forth. The librarian can choose topics that may fall into areas of some but not all areas of students' pre-existing expertise. This will allow those with expertise to demonstrate a different set of abilities than those without. The class, with librarian guidance, can walk through the steps of evaluating and corroborating information sources.

CHECK FOR UNDERSTANDING

The librarian asks the following questions:

- "Based on what everyone has said, what are the common ways you intuitively evaluate information?" Students then organize, through dialogue, the statements about evaluation into a checklist of related activities. The checklist typically includes standard criteria, in students' own language, for evaluating information (authority, accuracy, currency, etc.).

- "What's the difference between what you do to evaluate something in your area of expertise and what you do when you're not an expert?" Students reflect on the interview question and answer it again in light of the foregoing conversation. Students should be able to articulate the fact that in areas where they have expertise, they have no need to use such criteria explicitly, while in situations where they have little or developing expertise, there is more work to do.

- "What will you need to do to acquire intuitive judgment in new areas of life, such as your major in college, or your future career?" Connections should be made to the earlier interview question, "What did you have to do to acquire that expertise?"

INDEPENDENT PRACTICE

The librarian or instructor/professor can pair this workshop with an outside-of-class scaffolding activity that supports research paper writing, speech writing, or other student work. Students can be asked to maintain a research journal documenting their evaluation/corroboration activities as part of their assignment—create an annotated bibliography for their paper, speech, or project, etc.

ACKNOWLEDGMENTS

The author would like to acknowledge his colleagues for their continued discussion of and participation in the development of this exercise, particularly Jennifer Poggiali, for her helpful conversations about the exercise's structure.

Determining the Relevance and Reliability of Information Sources

Students critically evaluate information sources for relevance and reliability by evaluating, with their peers, sample sources of information for a given topic.

CONCEPT IN CONTEXT

This lesson provides beginning students with a checklist to get them thinking critically about information's origins, purpose, and complexity, but takes them into a deeper discussion about how to apply those evaluative criteria. Students struggle with the idea that both relevance and reliability of information are contextual and related to the information need at hand. They need to understand that voices of authority are not appointed but get their status from context. Information that is appropriate in one research situation will not necessarily work for another. Reliability and relevance are not mutually exclusive, nor are they totally dependent on one another; they are context-driven, and engaging students in conversation encourages them to develop an appreciation of the importance of the situation. As fits a lesson on context, it is not scripted, and the librarian must be prepared to stray from the lesson plan or answer unexpected questions.

> **Author**:   Nancy Fawley, Head, Library Liaison Program
> *University of Nevada Las Vegas*

Level: Basic
Estimated Time: 50–75 minutes

MATERIALS NEEDED

- In preparation for the class, the librarian selects a variety of resources that are related to the class's sample research topic. The topic can be developed by the librarian or suggested by the instructor. These resources should be a mix of scholarly journal articles, magazine or newspaper articles, blog posts, and general web content that are relevant and/or reliable sources.
- Access to a computer and links to previously selected articles to be evaluated.

- Links to the articles can be embedded in the class Blackboard site, provided in a Google Doc, or given to students on the board, etc. This exercise can be adapted for classes with no computer access by providing students with paper copies of the sources to be evaluated.
- Handout with a checklist to assist students in determining a source's relevance and reliability (*see Appendix or www.ala.org/ acrl/files/handouts.pdf*)

LEARNING GOALS

- Students will be able to differentiate between reliability and relevance of information.
- Students will understand the relationship between reliability and relevance.
- Students will use this understanding to select appropriate resources for their research topic.

ANTICIPATORY SET

Librarian Script:

Imagine you have just moved to town and you are looking for a doctor for a physical. Your options are:

- An internationally known, award-winning podiatrist who specializes in foot fungus
- A general practitioner in town who is affordable; he has recently been investigated for Medicare fraud
- Your aunt's best friend's general practitioner, who has been rated highly online
- Who do you choose? Why?

The students are likely to choose the third doctor, but the librarian helps students understand *why*. The best choice is relevant, reliable, and contextual.

LESSON OBJECTIVE STATED

Librarian Script: "Today we are going to look at sources of information to determine if they are appropriate for the research topic that we are using in class today. You will learn how to evaluate them according to relevance, reliability, and the context in which they are used."

INPUT/MODELING

The librarian leads the class in a discussion of a short article on a research topic using the following criteria. The librarian points out the importance of context for determining both.

Reliable:

- Is the author qualified to write about the topic? (Look at her or his credentials, experience, or organizational affiliations.)
- Does the URL reveal anything about the author or source?
- Is the author trying to sell something?
- Does the source reveal a bias?
- Is the information factual?
- Are there spelling, grammar or other typographical errors?
- Is the information current?

Relevant:

- Does the information relate to your topic or answer your question?
- Does the source meet the requirements of your assignment?
- Is the information at an appropriate level (not too elementary or advanced for your needs)?

GUIDED PRACTICE/CHECK FOR UNDERSTANDING

The librarian divides the class into groups, and each group is assigned a source to read. Students skim their source and consider reliability and relevance in the context of their research using the above-listed criteria. Each group reports their findings to the class. This is an opportunity for the librarian to clarify "muddy" points and misperceptions and emphasize areas of importance. A discussion on popular and scholarly articles is appropriate in this lesson, as well.

INDEPENDENT PRACTICE

If there is time at the end of the class, students can search the library's databases or discovery tool to find one reliable and relevant source for their research assignment.

METHODS OF ASSESSMENT

The librarian can assess through the class discussion of relevancy and reliability of each source. Possibly, the librarian can evaluate student bibliographies. Student learning can be assessed by evaluating the students' bibliographies for the relevance and reliability of the sources they used in their research assignment.

Establishing and Applying Evaluation Criteria

Students work together to generate and apply a set of evaluative criteria in order to determine the quality of a variety of information sources.

CONCEPT IN CONTEXT

Context is crucial when evaluating information. As expressed in the anticipatory set of this lesson, the amount of information available to students at the click of a mouse makes it increasingly important that they search creatively and be appropriately skeptical of what they find. When experienced researchers evaluate information, they make a number of assessments simultaneously, all within the context of a particular information need. They do this without consciously separating out the particulars. Students new to research can build proficiency by discussing the evaluative process and internalizing these criteria through practice. This lesson moves beyond the novice level. It asks students to consider what makes information and its creators authoritative outside the boundaries of traditional markers such as "peer-reviewed" or "scholarly." It acknowledges the wide range of information accessible to students and encourages them to consider their information need when making determinations of quality and authority.

> **Author**:   Steven Hoover, Learning Commons Librarian
> *Syracuse University Libraries, Syracuse, New York*

Level: Beginning to intermediate
Estimated Time: 30–45 minutes

MATERIALS NEEDED
- Instructor access to a computer/projector with sound
- An example video or description that provides a research context
- A whiteboard, chalkboard, or flipchart for recording student responses
- Context-relevant information resources to evaluate

- Student computer access is helpful but not required

LEARNING GOAL
- Students will be able to generate and apply evaluative criteria to a source of information in order to judge its value relative to a given need.

ANTICIPATORY SET
Librarian Script: "The amount of information at our disposal can be mind-boggling. Even when a library can't provide sources of information on a particular topic or information that will answer a particular question, the Internet almost certainly can. Because of this, we're rarely in a situation where we can't find information, but we are often in a situation where we need to decide if the information we've found is something we should use. Remember that not all information is of the same quality, and we need to be somewhat skeptical of what we find."

LESSON OBJECTIVES STATED
Librarian Script: "Today, we'll identify some of the characteristics of quality information, and we will practice evaluating sources based on these characteristics."

INPUT/MODELING
The librarian starts with a think/pair/share activity to identify a set of evaluative criteria. To do this, the librarian asks students to take three minutes to think of an answer to the following question on their own: "What are some characteristics of good or 'reliable' information?"

It is helpful for the librarian to model an example before the students begin the activity. The librarian might say, "One important characteristic might be the purpose of the author. Why are they writing, creating, or compiling this information? Is their purpose to inform, to persuade, to generate discussion, to entertain, etc.? We can use information created for any of these purposes, but we need to be careful because the purpose of the author has a strong influence on how they present information, deal with contradictions, the amount that they editorialize, and so on."

The librarian lets the students think for three minutes and jot down notes on their own. At the end of the three minutes, they are asked to form small groups, discuss their ideas for three additional minutes, and prepare to share with the entire class. After group discussions, the librarian should reconvene the class and ask groups to report out. During this discussion, the librarian creates a list of characteristics (evaluative criteria) on the board/flipchart, making sure to challenge, fill in gaps, or massage suggestions as needed. This can take anywhere between ten and fifteen minutes.

Criteria will depend on context and may include but are not limited to:

- Author credentials
- References
- Publication prestige
- Purpose of use
- Publication process
- Reliability
- Currency
- Relevance

CHECK FOR UNDERSTANDING/GUIDED PRACTICE

In order for students to apply the criteria they have identified, they need context. Video clips from *The Daily Show* or other programs that discuss current events work well because they can be timely and often deal with researchable topics. This lesson plan is based on a statement made during the 2012 U.S. presidential campaign, but any clip that deals with a researchable current event would work.

The librarian provides students with example materials to evaluate. Examples can include books, newspaper articles, magazine articles, academic journal articles, website printouts, government documents, legal briefs, and other primary source materials. Each should be problematic in some way, but not so problematic as to be an obvious candidate for rejection. For example, the librarian can choose a scholarly journal article that is tangentially related or highly technical, a tax filing for an organization that is authentic but difficult to interpret, a well-researched and credible webpage from an organization that students might not be familiar with (ProPublica, The Pew Research Center, etc.), a well-researched but highly biased article, etc. A set of possible examples is included below. Ask the students to decide, as a group, if they were working on a research project (perhaps the project for this class) on the topic depicted in the video, would they use the source they have been given, and why or why not? The groups must address as many of the criteria identified during the think/pair/share activity as possible, explain whether or not they would use the source based on their evaluation, and describe how they would use the source in their paper. Group responses provide excellent opportunities for formative assessment, especially if the librarian takes an active role in challenging their assertions.

EXAMPLE SET OF MATERIALS TO EVALUATE

Based on a video clip from *The Daily Show* (2:58 minutes) regarding Mitt Romney's campaign promise to cut government funding to public television:

> http://www.thedailyshow.com/watch/mon-october-8-2012/
> children-s-television-chop-shop

Sources Provided to Students:
(Note: Each source includes some information that could be shared with students concerning the method of creation, purpose, and/or intended audience in order to reinforce the idea that pieces of information, and their respective formats, have strong relationships to the processes that create them. Also, most of the sources are available online, negating a simplistic approach to evaluation based on the method of access.)

- "American Broadcasting: Muggings on Sesame Street," *The Economist*, March 11, 1995, 84–85.
  This is an article from a respected publication, written to inform an educated audience, created by editorial process, but a bit out of date.
- H.R. 68, 112th United States Congress (2011). "To Amend the Communications Act of 1934 to prohibit Federal Funding for the Corporation for Public Broadcasting after Fiscal Year 2013." http://thomas.loc.gov/cgi-bin/query/z?c112:H.R.68:.
  This is a primary source, created by legislative process for the purposes of lawmaking and documentation, so maybe not the most easily digestible or usable resource.

- Nazli Kibria and Jain Sonali, "Cultural Impacts of Sisimpur, Sesame Street, in Rural Bangladesh: Views of Family Members and Teachers," *Journal of Comparative Family Studies* 40, no. 1, (2009): 57–78.

  This is a peer-reviewed academic journal article about children's television, but with a narrowly-defined focus far outside the scope of the issue in question. It provides excellent information and analysis but not readily usable in this case.

- Corporation for Public Broadcasting, *IRS Form 990*, 2010. http://www.cpb.org/aboutcpb/financials/990/cpb_form990_fy10.pdf.

  This is another primary source, but perhaps even more difficult to use than the House Resolution. This was created for purposes of regulatory compliance, made available for reasons of transparency, but not exactly created for the purpose of informing anyone other than the IRS. Maybe a summary report containing some of the same information would be a better choice.

- Suevon Lee. "Big Bird Debate: How Much Does Federal Funding Matter to Public Broadcasting?" *ProPublica*, October 11, 2012. http://www.propublica.org/article/big-bird-debate-how-much-does-federal-funding-matter-to-public-broadcasting.

  This is a well-researched article with a plethora of references and links from a respected website whose mission is to provide the public with quality investigative journalism. Although the article lists a single author, it was likely subject to editorial review. There is absolutely nothing wrong with the article on the whole, but it could be mistaken for a source that is not credible if judged solely on its format. ProPublica has won two Pulitzer Prizes since 2010, no small feat.

METHODS OF ASSESSMENT

Formative assessments include group responses to the prompts from the think/pair/share and source evaluation activities, as well individual responses to questions and challenges from the librarian. Summative assessments vary depending on the situation but could include rubric-based analyses of bibliographies or annotated bibliographies created as part of a research project.

Non-Scholarly Formats as Research Tools

In this brief lesson, students examine examples of professional organization press releases and/or blog posts to gain insight into disciplinary writing. They are encouraged to think about how purpose, audience, and authority operate within these disciplinary conversations.

CONCEPT IN CONTEXT

Professional organization blogs, newsletter articles, and press releases are forms of writing within a discipline, and are every bit as appropriate as scholarly publications to gain insight into the pressing issues within a profession or discipline. Examining these formats and genres and the process of their production is instructive to a student entering the discourse of a field. Doing so prompts discussion in many possible areas, including audience and purpose, language/jargon, currency, and what constitutes authority. Looking at these non-scholarly publications can also lead to a greater understanding of other forms of disciplinary writing such as scholarly publications, trade publications, and books.

Overlapping Threshold Concept: This lesson also addresses the concept of *Information Creation as a Process*.

Author: Rachel M. Minkin, Head of Reference Services
Michigan State University, East Lansing

Level: Basic
Estimated time: 15–20 minutes

MATERIALS NEEDED

- Handout *(see Appendix or www.ala.org/acrl/files/handouts.pdf)*
- Student computers or printed copies of preselected press releases or professional organization blog posts
- Projector

LEARNING GOAL

- Students will identify and assess usefulness of forms of disciplinary writing other than scholarly journals, trade journals, books, etc.

ANTICIPATORY SET

Librarian Script: "Do you ever use non-scholarly sources for papers or projects? Why are they useful? Have you ever been told NOT to use non-scholarly sources?"

Note: This is an opportunity for the librarian to define or discuss scholarly/non-scholarly sources.

LESSON OBJECTIVE STATED

Librarian Script: "Today we're going to look at professional writing in different fields and think about how things like blog posts, newsletters, and press releases can help us understand a profession or discipline."

INPUT/MODELING

The librarian distributes or provides a URL to a blog post or press release chosen by the librarian. This should be from a professional association that is related to the discipline(s) of the class. The librarian asks students to consider the following questions (the librarian can hand these out, project them, or simply ask them verbally):

- What kind (genre) of writing is this?
- Who's interested in this text? Which majors? Which professionals?
- If we wanted to find out more on this topic, what words (or related terms and words) should we use to search for additional information?
- Thinking about your own major, what questions do you have for this author or about the writing?

After reading and considering these questions individually, the librarian facilitates a discussion with the following prompts:

- As a class, let's list the majors that would have students interested in this reading. (The intent here is to establish that many academic majors may overlap in disciplines.)
- Who is the author and/or the author's organization? (Here, the goal is to have students discuss the authority of the author.)

- What is the format of the writing? How does it differ from scholarly articles? How is the content related? Can you imagine a scholarly article about this topic? (The librarian guides the students to think about how these formats differ [the production, the audience] but are also related [in the content, and in issues that are important in practice and in theory].)
- Let's generate a list of keywords (and potential synonyms/related topics) present in the post/press release. (This establishes a common vocabulary one could use for further research on a topic.)
- Think about the post/press release in terms of your own proposed major and then pose questions of the writing or the author. (This establishes the fact that different disciplines think about the same type of information in different ways and with different values.)

Once students have engaged in this fairly quick exercise, the librarian can let students begin searching and evaluating information on their own. With the ideas of authority and the interdisciplinary nature of these sources already primed, students are likely to be more explicit about *why* they choose certain resources.

GUIDED PRACTICE/INDEPENDENT PRACTICE

This exercise is completed as an entire class as a warm-up to a more independent session later in the class. The librarian asks for answers/input. Later, students will complete this exercise independently with different information genres.

METHODS OF ASSESSMENT

Student-generated lists on the board, completed handout if used.

Scholarly/Non-Scholarly

Students examine a scholarly and a non-scholarly article to identify their characteristics and learn to appropriately incorporate the ideas of others into their own writing.

CONCEPT IN CONTEXT

New college students are often unfamiliar with the research process and the bodies of literature they will inevitably encounter in their classes. They must learn to identify not only the characteristics that scholarly literature exhibit, but also what determines the authority of those who produce it. Authority is not assigned. It depends on the context in which information is created, for whom it is created, and how it is used. To be an effective researcher, a student must be able to match pieces of information to their purposes of use in context. Convincing information is not always accurate information. Accurate but complicated information is not always useful in meaningful communication. Context is everything. In this lesson, students are introduced to scholarly and non-scholarly information and are asked to look critically at both. They are asked to consider the expertise of the authors and determine the suitability of each for use within various research contexts.

> **Author:**   Jo Angela Oehrli, Learning Librarian, Children's Literature Librarian
>
> Emily Hamstra, Learning Librarian, Kinesiology Librarian
> *University of Michigan, Ann Arbor*

Level: Basic/general education
Estimated Time: 20–30 minutes

MATERIALS NEEDED

- A scholarly and a non-scholarly article on the same topic. See notes for an option of two articles that work for this lesson.[1]
- If using the discovery tool version of this lesson (Option 1), students must have a computer with an Internet connection.

- Projection capability or handout *(see Appendix or www.ala.org/ acrl/files/handouts.pdf)*

LEARNING GOAL

Students will be able to identify the characteristics of a scholarly and a non-scholarly article in order to appropriately incorporate the ideas of others into their own writing.

ANTICIPATORY SET

Librarian Script:

> Imagine someone says to you, "I think we should cut the salaries of people in Congress. My Uncle Edward says they make way too much money and don't get anything done."
>
> Is this a convincing argument? Why or why not?
>
> Uncle Edward may seem like a reliable source to the person speaking, but no one else knows who Uncle Edward is. What are his credentials?
>
> What does convincing information look like? What are its characteristics?
>
> We might want to find a reputable or *scholarly* article that reports on congressional salaries by an expert or authority in the field. We might also want to know more about the work that Congress has completed. This information is the *evidence* that supports the argument. When you write a paper, you will need to use information that comes from reputable sources and/or authors.

LESSON OBJECTIVE STATED

Librarian Script: "Today we are going to look at some examples of different types of evidence to support an argument,[2] point, or thesis statement. Both of these examples are about the same topic. We are going to examine these examples and discuss how and when we could incorporate information from these articles into our writing."

INPUT/MODELING

Students obtain articles using one of the options below. They are encouraged to familiarize themselves with the article by reading a paragraph or two of each article and skimming through the rest. They are asked to consider each article's audience, subject, author, and structure.

The librarian should project or distribute a handout with the following questions as a guide for students:

1. Who wrote the article?
2. Who is the audience? Who reads articles like these?
3. What are the characteristics of these articles?
4. For what purpose might this article be used?

Option 1: Discovery Tool

Students are given the citations to two articles. (For article options, see an example at the end of the lesson.) Using the library's discovery tool, students search for and download both articles.

Option 2: Articles Provided

Students divide into pairs. Each student in the pair is given one of the articles. The librarian gives students time to look over their article. After a few minutes, they will trade articles with their partners.

GUIDED PRACTICE/CHECK FOR UNDERSTANDING

The librarian has students discuss the questions with a partner, addressing the following:

- The credentials of the authors
- The audience for each article (For example, in the trade publication *Firehouse*, the audience is fire fighters)
- Characteristics should include the date of the articles, the writing style, what they notice about the structure of the articles, references, and images
- The difference between scholarly and non-scholarly writing

After the small group discussion, the librarian leads a whole-class discussion, making sure to include the following points:

"When might it be appropriate to look for materials from non-scholarly sources? Scholarly sources?"

Non-Scholarly:

- Add a "human element" or interesting view
- Get an easy-to-understand overview of a topic
- Define or explain the history of a topic
- Refer to a specific work of art or literature

Scholarly:

- Quote study results or statistics to support a thesis statement
- Determine the validity of experiment or research
- Explain a topic that is technical or specific to a profession
- Refer to a specific work of art or literature

INDEPENDENT PRACTICE

If time allows, the librarian can give students another pair of articles and repeat the exercise.

ASSESSMENT (OPTIONAL)

If time allows, students complete a one-minute paper. The librarian asks students to describe how non-scholarly articles could be used in a paper about congressional salaries. They could then describe how scholarly articles could be used in the same paper.

NOTES

1. Suggested articles for discussion:
   — Petya Eckler and Yusuf Kalyango, "International Journalists' Expectations from the US Media Coverage of Hurricane Katrina," *Journalism* 11, no. 3 (2010): 277–292.
   — Harvey Eisner, "Hurricane Katrina," *Firehouse* 30, no.10 (2005): 44–50.

2. Throughout this book, the term *argument* refers to the subject matter of a student's scholarly output. It is not meant to refer to an exchange of opposing views or rhetorical tool for persuasion.

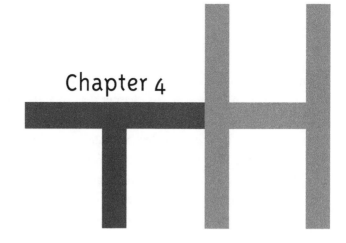

Chapter 4

Information Creation as a Process

INFORMATION IS PUBLISHED and distributed as a result of a wide variety of purposes and processes. In a pre-digital world, the way that information consumers interacted with information was shaped largely by the physical manifestation of the information. The physical "package" signaled to users the difference in the nature of the information contained within. This may, to some extent, have included an awareness or knowledge of the process that it took to create the final product, though this process would still require explanation to students. With digital information objects, the object may no longer be physical. It is a construct based on the process by and purpose for which it was created. This presents a challenge to the novice information user. How is one to know the difference between the digital version of an article from a weekly magazine and the digital version of an article from a scholarly, peer-reviewed journal?

With the advent of digital publishing, there are still a multitude of processes that underlie the creation of information objects. What is different is that the digital manifestations sometimes do not cue the user in to the fact that they are, indeed, different types of information. In order to appreciate the timeliness, accuracy, complexity, and other attributes of information, people need to understand the purpose and processes behind its creation. Two lessons in this chapter deal directly with the information life cycle. Xan Goodman's examines the information generated by one event over the course of a year to demonstrate to students the many purposes and processes driving the creation of different formats of information, from social media comments to scholarly articles. By viewing various information items on the same subject, students can become familiar with the characteristics of different information products. Another lesson, by Toni Carter and Todd Aldridge, engages students in a discussion of rigor and its relation to format. Scrutinizing the reasons behind knowledge creation helps students become more discerning users of the information they encounter.

While teaching students, librarians ideally are able to peel away their assumptions about what students know (or do not know) about the process of information creation. Beyond this, librarians need to be aware of the evolving landscape of information distribution and access, and the realities of how students find information. Discovery tools strip away the characteristics that once made distinctive differences in format recognizable. It is imperative, then, that students understand how and why information is created so they understand what they see.

The ease of digital publishing has enabled more people to engage in scholarship via self- publication in venues such as blogs, digital white papers, and podcasts. These information products, while lacking the rock-solid authority of traditional peer review, are undeniably contributing to the vitality of scholarly conversations. At the same time, these contributions to scholarship call for the need to critically evaluate information. (This is addressed in chapter 3, *Authority is Constructed and Contextual.*) Dani Brecher's lesson about using sources as evidence discusses this idea that limiting research to scholarly databases excludes a potential wealth of information resources for students; the lesson explores how the information in different manifestations is useful to scholars in different ways, based on the processes that resulted in their creation.

These lessons help librarians explain how the creation of information and the reasons for its dissemination are the underlying determinants of its value in research. Familiar formats change, distinctions blur, and new formats establish themselves. Librarians can use these lessons, alter them, and keep the conversation going.

Using Sources to Support a Claim

The purpose of this lesson is to demonstrate to students that support for statements made in academic writing may come in different formats, not just scholarly journal articles. Depending on the topic, more than one information product might be appropriate for the information need.

CONCEPT IN CONTEXT

Students are often told to limit their research to scholarly or peer-reviewed journal articles even when researching a topic that is likely to have been written about in other information formats, such as newspaper articles, online magazines, or blogs. The idea that there is a single standard for suitability is an easy one to fall back on in the classroom. There is no formula for "good" information, and while pointing students in the direction of certain sources makes it likely that they will find scholarly information, doing so obscures for them the notion that quality information is all around them. For students who have never handled an actual print journal, there is little to distinguish the information within its digital counterpart from what they have encountered elsewhere online.

Limiting research to scholarly journal articles implies that quality information can only be found in scholarly databases, when in fact scholarly conversations are going on everywhere, growing and multiplying faster than ever. A student researching a topic such as the one described in this lesson is apt to encounter difficulty and frustration trying to locate appropriate scholarly journal articles. Information is created for all kinds of reasons, in all kinds of ways. Peer review is designed to safeguard accuracy, but it takes time. New information disseminated through less traditional means is not necessarily less accurate but requires thorough evaluation and may not be acceptable in certain contexts. Understanding how and why information is created and how it is disseminated enables students to identify the best places to locate information and evaluate its value for their research.

Overlapping Threshold Concept: This lesson also addresses the concept *Authority is Constructed and Contextual.*

Author: Dani Brecher, Information Literacy and Learning Technologies Coordinator
Claremont Colleges Library, Claremont, California

Level: Basic/general education
Estimated Time: 50–60 minutes

MATERIALS NEEDED

- Copies of article excerpts. These can include for example, a blog post, a review, a magazine article, a newspaper article or editorial, or a scholarly journal article. The topic used in this lesson is the English band Radiohead, but another topic can be substituted.
- Handout *(See Appendix or www.ala.org/acrl/files/handouts.pdf)*

LEARNING GOAL

Students will understand that there are many different factors to consider when selecting an appropriate source for an assignment and that the factors may vary according to type of information need.

ANTICIPATORY SET

To begin the class the librarian can ask students about research papers they have written before, most likely in high school, specifically asking: "Were you asked to support a statement or claim with supporting evidence?"; "What kinds of evidence did those assignments require, and where did you look for it?"

The librarian may mention that while some research paper assignments in college have explicit instructions to use only scholarly sources, in some cases the only parameter will be to use appropriate sources. The librarian should ask, "What do you think that means?" If appropriate, the librarian may want to discuss the concept of scholarly versus popular before proceeding.

LESSON OBJECTIVE STATED

Librarian Script:

In college, research assignments usually carry a high burden of proof, requiring you to justify your position with appropriate and compelling sources of information. Just because an article is published in a scholarly journal doesn't necessarily mean that it is the best source for your paper. In today's class we are going to broadly explore the types of information that might be available about a particular research topic, and then consider which, if any, of these types of information would lend support to our research statement or claim.

Today we are going to consider the record album *Hail to the Thief* by the English rock band Radiohead and look at some information relating to it. We will look at one source together as a class and then we will break into groups. Each group will examine a different source and report back to the class as a whole.

INPUT/MODELING

The librarian will ask the students to read a short newspaper article[1] about a Radiohead album and use it as an example to discuss how a particular source of information was created (the processes of researching, writing, editing, and publishing) and its potential value as evidence to support a particular statement or claim. The librarian will lead a discussion with the class, based on the questions asked on the worksheet. Potential questions to explore include:

- What generally is the article about?
- For what purpose was it written?
- What was the process used to create the article; e.g., how long did it take the author to research and write it? Was it edited or reviewed? Who published it?
- If it contains factual information, do you think it is accurate?

Then the librarian will introduce two different claims suggested by the source. These claims can be on a handout or projected on a screen:

Claim 1: Radiohead's album, *Hail to the Thief*, was inspired by not only the political environment of its time, but also by Thom Yorke's (principal songwriter for Radiohead) interest in earlier 20th century political poets.

Claim 2: Public response to Radiohead's *Hail to the Thief* was colored by the public's strong opinion and memory of the band's previous albums.

The librarian asks the class:

"Can you find any support in this article for either of these claims?"

The librarian will then guide a discussion about whether the newspaper article could be used to bolster either of these claims. Even though the article is not scholarly, it could be used to support Claim 2. The librarian will discuss how the core argument of the article, that only schoolchildren could fully appreciate the Radiohead album, relates to the claim. The librarian may also discuss how the sarcastic tone of the article also relates to the claim.

GUIDED PRACTICE

Students will then be divided into groups where each is given an additional reading on the topic of *Hail to the Thief*, including a blog post,[2] a review,[3] a magazine profile,[4] a newspaper editorial,[5] and a scholarly journal article.[6] Students will be asked to review their reading and complete part 1 of the worksheet together, discussing their answers.

CHECK FOR UNDERSTANDING

A volunteer from a group who looked at each type of article will report back to the class with a brief summary of their article.

INDEPENDENT PRACTICE

Students will be asked to decide if their source could be used to support Claim 1 and or Claim 2 using Part 2 and 3 of the worksheet. For example, the blog post might be appropriate for a paper on public response to Radiohead, but be completely inappropriate for a paper on Radiohead's influences. These two claims call for two very different kinds of evidence.

Students will then report to the class with their conclusions, selecting one direct quote from the article that supports their decision.

NOTES

1. Rob Harvilla, "Radiohead Rorschach," *East Bay Express*, September 17, 2003, http://www.eastbayexpress.com/oakland/radiohead-rorschach/Content?oid=1071613.

2. Jazz Monroe, "An Overlooked Masterpiece" *Drowned in Sound* (blog), June 14, 2013, http://drownedinsound.com/in_depth/4146516-all-hail-the-culturati-fighting-over-radioheads-hail-to-the-thief.

3. Chris Ott, review of *Hail to the Thief*, by Radiohead, *Pitchfork*, June 9, 2003, http://pitchfork.com/reviews/albums/6658-hail-to-the-thief/.

4. Spin Staff, "Fitter Happier: Radiohead Return," *Spin*, June 29, 2003, http://www.spin.com/articles/fitter-happier-radiohead-return/.

5. Brad Kava, "Radiohead's Latest Goes to Show How Some Music Merits a Second—or Third or Fourth—Chance," *San Jose Mercury News*, January 14, 2004.

6. Kate Livett, "Thieves and Fascists: The Politics of Abjection in Radiohead's Hail to the Thief (The Gloaming)," *Australian Humanities Review* 41 (Feb. 2007). http://www.australianhumanitiesreview.org/archive/Issue-February-2007/Livett.html.

Information Life Cycle

This lesson asks students to evaluate information they use for their college writing assignments, such as newspapers, scholarly journal articles, etc., through the lenses of format and rigor by introducing them to the information life cycle.

CONCEPT IN CONTEXT

The connection between format and quality of information is not apparent to novice researchers. Students just beginning to do research are learning about the importance of evaluating the information they discover, but their understanding of the information life cycle is probably limited. Here, the librarian fosters student awareness of the different information formats and how the process behind their creation determines their shape, content, and quality, or *rigor*, the term used in this lesson. Students examine articles from a variety of sources and think about the time it takes to create the information in each. This obvious examination of time spent on production requires students to think critically about the information they encounter: why it was created, for whom, and what effect the time element has on the depth, accuracy, and overall impact of its content. Can we compare the rigor of an article in a journal to that of a newspaper article? Are there degrees of rigor within each format? This activity engages students with the content in a way that compels them to consider the format of information each time they consider using it in their work.

Authors: Toni M. Carter, Library Instruction Coordinator

Todd Aldridge, English Graduate Teaching Assistant
Auburn University, Auburn, Alabama

Level: Basic/general education
Estimated Time: 50–60 minutes

MATERIALS NEEDED

- Five stations are set up throughout the classroom prior to the start of the class. These can be whiteboards or large pieces of paper taped to the wall.

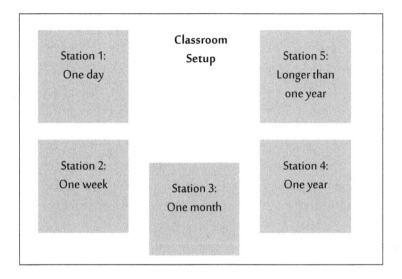

- Preselected current news story or topic relevant to the class being taught
- Preselected information sources representing five sources of information in different formats about the news story or topic (as described in the Input/Modeling section below); preferably there will be at least two options for each format, e.g., two different sources that could be placed at station 1 and so on
- Worksheet (*see Appendix or www.ala.org/acrl/files/handouts.pdf*)
- Post-it notes
- Internet access
- Time frames matching the stations are written or projected on boards for student reference (e.g., one day, one week, one month, one year, longer than a year)

LEARNING GOAL

Students will learn that information is produced and disseminated in different formats and that the accuracy and thoroughness (rigor) of information is often related to the length of time it takes to produce the information, its final form, and the way it is shared with others.

ANTICIPATORY SET

After introductions, the librarian instructs students to self-select in pairs or small groups, and each group is assigned a source relating to the pre-selected news story or topic (e.g., a newspaper, a magazine, a scholarly journal, a book). The librarian can either provide paper copies or direct students where to find the source online.

Students are given time to review the source and fill out the worksheet. They then are asked to make their best estimate as to when the source was published in relationship to the event it describes, with reference to the time frames written on the board. The librarian instructs them to write the title and/or citation of their source on a Post-it note and then post it on the station they believe represents the appropriate answer.

(In the case of time limitations, assign each group question #1, along with only two or three of the additional questions, making sure all questions are covered by at least one group.)

LESSON OBJECTIVE STATED

The librarian brings the class back together and tells students, "You each have had the opportunity to examine one source of information about [topic]. Today we are going to look at different types of information sources that all concern the same topic and examine how the format of these sources changes over time. You will be asked to assess and explain the qualities of the source assigned to you."

INPUT/MODELING

Starting at Station 1 (one day), the librarian then leads a class discussion about the sources posted at the various stations, asking students who reviewed these sources to elaborate on the answers on their worksheet. During this discussion, the librarian introduces the concept of rigor as an important characteristic of information products.

Librarian Script: "What is rigor? It is the quality of thoroughness, accuracy, and strictness of a source. This can include the author's credentials, how the author got the information he/she is writing about, and who reviewed the source prior to its publication."

For example, Station 1 could consist of online news, newspaper articles, and possibly blog posts. The librarian asks students to define the general characteristics, style, and form of these formats.

Students may not know all of the relevant characteristics, so the librarian will have to lead the conversation. Prompts for the librarian can include:

Online news/newspaper articles:
- written by a reporter or journalist
- written for a general audience
- not peer-reviewed
- can consist of facts and opinions about a topic

Blog posts:
- can be written by novice or expert
- aimed toward a general audience, but could be focused

Station 2 (one week) could have longer newspaper articles, weekly magazine articles, etc.

Station 3 (one month) could have monthly magazine articles; longer online articles.

Station 4 (one year) could have a journal article.

Here the librarian can ask students to consider scholarly journal articles by asking the following: "You are often asked to find and use them as references in your research papers. What are the characteristics of that information product? Is there any difference between on-line and print journals?"

Journal article:
- written by an expert in the field
- peer-reviewed
- written for a scholarly audience
- often contain results of original research

Station 5 (longer than one year) could include books and encyclopedia entries.

GUIDED PRACTICE

Students search a library database or the Internet to find two sources of comparable rigor and format on the same topic. The librarian and class instructor circulate throughout the room assisting students as needed.

(Optional: Students enter the citations of the sources they find in a Google form created for this purpose by the librarian. The librarian can review students' responses after class for assessment purposes.)

INDEPENDENT PRACTICE

Outside of the library session, students independently locate two sources of comparable format and rigor. Students then apply ideas from the library session and justify their choices in a short writing assignment. Librarians and class instructors can evaluate the writing assignments together in order to assess learning outcomes from these activities.

Tracing Information over Time

This lesson introduces students to the information cycle by taking them through the creation of information related to a popular culture event that is familiar to students.

CONCEPT IN CONTEXT

The information cycle is generally understood to mean the production of various formats of information over time. By understanding that information is created, produced, and disseminated within various time constraints, students will recognize what types of information they can expect to find on any particular topic and have a better understanding of where to find it. Students who are looking for information on a very recent news event or topic will realize that the only information available may be in online newspapers, blogs, or social media, and this information may not be completely reliable. On the other hand, students writing a research paper on a disciplinary topic will expect to find information on this subject in a variety of formats, from magazine articles, to scholarly journals, to books.

Students who understand that information is produced and disseminated in a variety of ways at different points following an event are better prepared to critically evaluate the value of the information that they find and determine its usefulness for their information need.

Overlapping Threshold Concept: This lesson also addresses the concept *Authority is Constructed and Contextual.*

Author: Xan Goodman, Health and Life Sciences Liaison
Librarian
University of Nevada, Las Vegas

Level: Basic
Estimated Time: 50–60 minutes

MATERIALS NEEDED

- Internet access
- Optional link to video explaining information life cycle
- At least one example of a popular culture information event, old

enough to have worked through the information cycle, but one
that students will be familiar with, such as:

- The circumstances surrounding Michael Jackson's death
  in June 2009
- The case of the intimate partner violence between
  Rihanna and Chris Brown that occurred in February
  2009 (This example may be upsetting for students.
  Librarians should be aware of this and approach the topic
  of domestic violence with sensitivity.)

- A PowerPoint or other type of presentation containing preselected examples of information generated about the selected
  information events corresponding to each of the five time periods of the information cycle. The background color of each
  slide should be one of five colors corresponding to the index
  cards described below.
- Five color-coded index cards that each contain one question.
  Prior to class, the librarian asks five students to assist during
  the discussion. Each of these five students is given a colored
  index card containing one question. They are directed to ask
  that question when they see the color matching their card on a
  slide. The following are suggested questions which the librarian
  should feel free to adapt for his or her own purposes or to focus
  the class in different ways:

1. How accurate do you think the information in social media is?
   (For slide 1)
2. Are newspaper articles scholarly sources? Why or why not?
   (For slide 2)
3. How is the process of publishing magazines different from
   newspapers? (For slide 3)
4. What is a scholarly journal and what is the process by which it
   is published? (For slide 4)
5. What is the value of information published in an encyclopedia?
   In a book? (For slide 5)

LEARNING GOALS

- Students will be able to define the information cycle.
- Students will learn the five parts of the information cycle using a popular culture example and learn what information sources fit where in the cycle.
- Students will understand how information flows through the cycle which will allow them to better select sources for their class projects.

ANTICIPATORY SET/LESSON OBJECTIVE STATED

Librarian Script: "Today we are going to talk about how information is generated and more specifically about what is called the information cycle. At the end of this instruction session, you will understand how information is generated about topics over the course of time. This knowledge will help you identify appropriate information sources for your class assignment."

INPUT/MODELING

The librarian will begin class by leading a discussion on the information cycle. This can begin with an optional short online tutorial on the information cycle if desired. There are a number available from academic librarians on the Internet, including one from the University of Illinois at Urbana-Champaign Libraries at http://www.library.illinois.edu/diglit/tutorials/InfoCycle/InformationCycle.html.

The author of this lesson has defined the information cycle as consisting of five approximate periods:

- The day of an event
- A day to a week following the event
- A month following the event
- Months after the event
- Years after the event

The librarian introduces the periods of the information life cycle and asks students to discuss each through the presentation of a PowerPoint or Prezi. During this presentation, students who have the color-coded index cards will read the card when the corresponding color is displayed on a slide. The librarian can answer the question or can facilitate class discussion by soliciting student responses.

For example, the librarian will tell students that they are going to look at the information cycle of an event that they are all likely to be familiar with (death of Michael Jackson or other predetermined subject). The librarian will then bring up a slide showing a clip of one or more of the resources and lead a class discussion on the following:

Slide 1 What types of information were released the day Michael Jackson died?

- Television, Internet, social media, radio, Twitter, Facebook (slide may contain visual of a TV broadcast or Internet post)

Slide 2 In a day to a week following his death:

- Newspapers, more in-depth on-line articles, blogs (slide may contain newspaper article)

Slide 3 In the month following his death:

- Popular magazines (slide may contain cover of *People* Magazine)

Slide 4 In the months after his death:

- Television documentaries, longer, in-depth essays and articles

Slide 5 In the year(s) after his death:

- Academic articles, books, encyclopedia articles, feature-film documentaries, government reports

Students can be asked to think of other formats of information that could be generated during each stage of the information cycle.

GUIDED PRACTICE

The class is divided into groups or pairs. The librarian introduces another topic to the entire class or has several different topics prepared and assigns each group/pair a different topic. Each group/pair is given the task of finding an item of information about their topic and discussing how it fits into the information cycle. One student from each group/pair will be asked to demonstrate to the class how they searched for their item, what they found, and where this item fits into the information cycle.

The librarian can use several different popular culture events for this exercise, and one or more of these examples can be events that are more recent or very recent and which may not have gone through the entire information cycle. This will further reinforce students' understanding of the concept.

Chapter 5

Searching as Strategic Exploration

IMAGINE ENTERING A forest on a path. As you pass through the first tower-
ing trees of the forest and continue down the path, you see that it has other
paths branching off. One leads into a small meadow filled with colorful
butterflies. A few hundred feet later, you stumble across a perfect climb-
ing tree with branches leading high into the canopy. Another path leads
down a hill to a stream surrounded with gorgeous mosses. Not everything
is sweetness and light, though; you sometimes hear the terrifying screams
of wild animals in the distance, and in yet another part of the woods you
smell a festering toxic bog. You quickly realize that the possibilities for
exploring this forest are endless, and the path you choose will influence
your journey immensely.

    When a researcher sets out to answer a question, s/he is embarking
on a journey. Ideally, this journey is fueled by inquiry and a desire to know.
Realistically, many students are searching for one or two items; they want
to step in the forest, collect a few specimens, then get back home. However,
librarians can encourage students to view their searching as strategic exploration, which can help them understand some of the truths about searching for
information that may not be readily apparent to novices. For instance, viewing

the search as iterative can help students see the value in trying searches in slightly different ways, or using different search tools. Students also need to know that there is no one right path. There are many routes to find useful information that informs one's understanding of a problem or question, and sometimes, explorers discover that the answer they wanted does not exist.

As students become more information literate and more familiar with the research in their disciplines , they become more able to access information both effectively and efficiently. A research plan that identifies the necessary search language (i.e., keywords, related terms, and discipline-specific vocabulary) will help them target the needed information rather than wander about, hoping to stumble upon it. Students can also be encouraged to be familiar with discipline-specific databases and their features, such as Boolean operators and database limiters. It is not necessary that they know the names for such strategies. They must, however, understand how and why information is organized and located, which means understanding the underlying organization of a system and the language used within it.

The lessons in this chapter help librarians approach teaching students about the explorative aspects of searching in many ways. In "Framing a Topic for Library Research" by Melissa Browne, Caitlin Plovnick, Cathy Palmer, and Richard Caldwell, students consider possible audiences, purposes, and conversations around a topic. Putting a topic in a context helps students find sources about it that will, in turn, help them understand the topic with more nuance and accuracy. This lesson also guides students to try multiple searches, allowing for search strategies to morph and adapt as students learn more about their topics. In Melissa Langridge's "Password: Keyword Edition," the librarian stages a game-show-style activity where students explore the vocabulary of a topic or discipline by generating synonyms and related concepts. This prepares students to approach topics with flexibility and a knowledge that it may take multiple attempts to arrive at useful keywords. Jenny Fielding's lesson "Context through Citation" helps students see how citations provide a roadmap for other scholarly articles that address an issue or problem. The lesson also helps students mine articles for vocabulary that informs their choice of keywords, preparing students to search for and find further information. This chapter includes a variety of other approaches that can be adapted for many students' and librarians' needs, and will help students start exploring.

From Nothing to Something: Transforming the "Failed" Search

Students learn that a failed search does not end the exploration process and they develop strategies to continue their research after encountering obstacles. This lesson relies on feedback from students and requires a certain amount of flexibility and readiness on the part of librarians to respond to a range of search outcomes.

CONCEPT IN CONTEXT

Expert researchers are able to navigate the complex information landscape, from databases with specialized vocabularies to the not-so-well-defined online environment of social media. What sets them apart from novice researchers, though, is more than knowledge of the available resources. Expert researchers can overcome obstacles and learn from unproductive searches. They are flexible and skilled enough to look elsewhere and attentive enough to spot useful information when and wherever it appears. Students do need to learn to use sophisticated university databases. They also need to recognize that quality information doesn't exist only behind a paywall. But, the search for information is seldom as straightforward as we would like, and students will encounter difficulty along the way. How they handle that difficulty is the true measure of their learning. This lesson gets to the place where students may find themselves stuck—where they hit a figurative wall—and shows them that failure is okay. It addresses the search strategies and discovery tools students need to employ to recognize the possible reasons for setbacks and continue their research. When students are no longer intimidated by failure, they can begin to engage in real exploration.

Author: Ika Datig, Reference and Research Librarian
New York University, Abu Dhabi

Level: Intermediate
Estimated Time: 30–40 minutes

MATERIALS NEEDED

- Instructor computer and projector screen
- Whiteboard

- For independent searching, students should have access to a computer

LEARNING GOALS

- Students will learn that a failed search (one that retrieves no results or irrelevant results) is not something to be afraid of. Instead, failure is an inevitable and helpful part of the exploration process.
- Students will learn to analyze a problematic search and come up with a solution.

ANTICIPATORY SET

Librarian Script: "In your classes, have you ever been unable to find information for your assignments? Have you ever heard someone else say, 'There's nothing in the library on my topic'? Besides getting frustrated, how do you deal with failure? What does failure look like?"

LESSON OBJECTIVE STATED

Librarian Script: "Today you are going to search for information on a topic and learn what to do when you don't find the information you're looking for. Failed searches aren't the end of your exploration. Together we'll work to learn from our mistakes and keep searching."

INPUT/MODELING

Prior to the class, the librarian prepares one or more searches on a discipline-related topic, incorporating one or more of the following failed search triggers:

- Too narrow or focused
- Natural language, rather than targeted key words
- Too many words in a single search, or a search written as a sentence
- A search done in an incorrect/irrelevant database
- A search containing misspellings

The class examines the search results together, and critiques the effectiveness of the search. When a search 'fails,' the class works together to determine why it has happened.

The librarian divides the class into groups (groups of 3–4 are optimal). Each group is given a research question related to their assignment or course content. In their groups, the students brainstorm keywords related to the research question and write them down. Each group (or representative) comes to the instructor's computer to perform a search in front of the class. Searches should be split between the library catalog and the database.

Rather than introduce some of the potential problems before the search, like the need for targeted language or Boolean operators, this lesson allows the students to experience the common sticking places for novice searchers in order to recognize, understand, and overcome them. They are likely to include:

- Keyword problems: Overcoming the impulse towards natural language searching; recognizing the need for synonyms; learning academic jargon and using thesauri (when appropriate)
- Adapting keywords according to the resource: Broad searches in the library catalog vs. greater detail in a database
- Considering the information cycle: Is the topic too 'new' to be covered in books or scholarly journal articles? How can students use the available scholarly information?
- Unanticipated information found: What can be learned along the way about one's topic that could inform (or alter) one's search?; How to broaden, narrow, or switch focus of topic

With each "failure," students see how a wrong-footed search is just a temporary setback, and in fact is often very useful in learning about their research topic and the organization of information. The librarian reminds students that librarians are available to help them whenever they "fail" in the future.

GUIDED PRACTICE

Students are given time to search independently using their own research topics, and to raise their hands whenever they "fail." Failures can be addressed by the instructor/professor, librarian, or peers (optimal).

Context through Citation

By reading and identifying the textual embedding of citations in a scholarly article, students learn to follow a scholarly conversation and search strategically for additional information on a topic.

CONCEPT IN CONTEXT

Citations are standard fare for librarians, but citation instruction typically focuses on mechanics. When students see the work of one researcher cited in the work of another, they can begin to recognize the connectedness of scholarly writing; they are able to conceptualize the conversation. In this lesson, citations are used as signifiers within a scholarly narration, teaching students to use the information they have to find additional, related information.

This lesson comprises two overlapping threshold concepts, *Searching as Strategic Exploration*, and *Scholarship as Conversation*. For students to become adept researchers, they need to be able to identify a variety of information systems, and they need to recognize the clues contained within information artifacts that may lead them to new places to search. Librarians refer to this approach as "citation chasing" or "citation tracking." This lesson provides the conceptual explanation for what makes it an effective search strategy and way to understand how authors follow and add to the scholarly conversation. It provides a solid foundation on which to scaffold database or controlled-vocabulary instruction.

Overlapping Threshold Concept: This lesson also address the concept *Scholarship as Conversation*.

Author: Jenny Fielding, Reference Librarian
Northern Essex Community College, Haverhill, Massachusetts

Level: Introductory to intermediate, appropriate for introductory course or research methods course within a discipline
Estimated Time: 45–60 minutes

MATERIALS NEEDED

- Copies of suggested article or short article in discipline
- Access to online library searching tool

LEARNING GOALS

- Students will learn to identify signals in scholarly literature pointing them to additional information in the form of narrative signifiers and in-text citations.
- Students will learn how to follow textual features to related citation in bibliography.
- Students will understand how to use citation information to locate articles.
- Students will recognize the purpose of a citation as it relates to contextual information.

ANTICIPATORY SET

Librarian Script: "Many of your assignments require that you use multiple scholarly sources. How often do you search databases and feel like there is very little on your topic? Or you find too much and have trouble choosing what's really relevant? By understanding how scholarly articles 'hook together,' you'll be able to find related useful information much more easily."

LESSON OBJECTIVE STATED

Librarian Script: "Today, we are going to read part of a scholarly article together and then use the clues left by the author to track down the information used to make a point. Once we figure out how that information connects to other information, we can find more sources on this topic."

INPUT/MODELING

A copy of a scholarly article is distributed to the class. The article cited below about proactivity and "morningness" works well for this lesson, although another short, scholarly article can be used.

Christoph Randler, "Proactive People are Morning People," *Journal of Applied Social Psychology*, 39, no.12 (2009): 2787-2797.

GUIDED PRACTICE

A volunteer student is chosen to read the abstract aloud. The class is asked to paraphrase the purpose of the study, and unfamiliar words are explained. Discussion topics:

- Why an abstract is helpful
- How understanding the author's point helps us to read the entire article

Another student is asked to read the second paragraph aloud. This almost always results in the student skipping the in-text citations. Discussion topics:

- Why they skipped them (or, if they didn't, how it interrupted the narrative flow)
- How citations act as "stop signs"—places the author tells the reader to make note of related information

The librarian will then pull out an individual sentence or sentences from this paragraph, and repeat the paraphrasing question to the students, reinforcing two points:

- The ideas are not the author's ideas—they are the ground work s/he consulted for this study (as the students, themselves, will consult and reference sources for their papers)
- The in-text citations point the way to the author's sources of information

An in-text citation is chosen and identified in the bibliography. Discuss:

- There may be more than one article by an author in the bibliography. How do we choose the right one? What does the fact that this person wrote more than one article on this topic tell us?

The librarian leads the class in analyzing the citation. What is the article title? What is the journal title? (Depending on the level of the class and time available, a brief review of citation style may be added here.)

The librarian models how to "follow" the citation and find the cited article via the appropriate library tool. Together, examine the new abstract. Discuss:

- Does this article relate? How would this help me if this were the topic of my paper?
- This article also has a bibliography, so the information trail continues, broadening the context and placing the ideas within the wider discipline.

INDEPENDENT PRACTICE

Students are given the opportunity to find another source of their choice from the bibliography. As possible common obstacles arise, discussion points can include:

- How to tell the difference between citations for different types of sources (book vs. article) and where to search for each
- Why some articles are not available online
- Access to non-library resources

What is a Database?

In this lesson, students explore a database that they may not even think of as a database (Flickr) and reflect on the way that it is designed to help users find photos. They then relate this familiar database to an academic database. Through the comparison, they become more comfortable with academic databases, and more aware of how to make the structure of a database work for them.

CONCEPT IN CONTEXT

Students' sense of curiosity and eagerness to discover information about topics that they care about should be the main feature of searching, not their discomfort with or confusion about the mechanics of databases. This lesson eases the transition between being a casual user of everyday databases (like Flickr, iTunes, or shopping websites) and becoming an academic library researcher who is comfortable and confident using proprietary and scholarly databases. Once this barrier is removed, a student can focus more on the exploration capabilities of the databases, rather than the minutia of operating them.

A successful search for information is usually iterative. It requires tenacity, curiosity, and flexibility. Before a student is an adept searcher, s/he may conceive of the search for information as a one-step search that must be done in "the right" place. With that approach, there may be too much pressure placed on that search to be exactly right. This lesson reinforces the need for trying searches in different places and in different ways, and builds on students' likely understanding of less pressure-laden (non-academic) searches. This exercise also helps students understand that flexibility and adaptability benefit their searches.

Authors: Samantha Godbey, Education Librarian, Assistant Professor

Sue Wainscott, STEM Librarian, Assistant Professor

Xan Goodman, Health and Life Sciences Liaison Librarian
University of Nevada, Las Vegas

Level: Basic/general education
Estimated Time: 30–50 minutes

MATERIALS NEEDED

- Whiteboard, paper, or other virtual place for brainstorming (for example, Padlet.com)
- Screenshots of databases to be distributed via handouts or project on screen
- Student computers with Internet access
- Copies of Exit Survey (*see Appendix or www.ala.org/acrl/files/handouts.pdf*)

LEARNING GOALS

- Students will be aware of the underlying structures and common features of databases. Students will recognize the transferability of search strategies between popular and academic databases.
- Students will become more confident using academic databases.

ANTICIPATORY SET

The librarian invites the students to brainstorm by asking, "When you hear the word 'database,' what comes to mind?"

As students answer, the librarian puts the answers into categories that are laid out on the white board: Description/Definition, Examples, and Other. The librarian explains to students that "Other" might include related words or emotions that they associate with databases.

Alternatively, the students can brainstorm online using a wall on padlet.com to allow multiple students to synchronously contribute to a document from their computer workstations.

When you hear the word "database," what comes to mind?		
Description/Definition	Examples	Other

After a few minutes of brainstorming, the class debriefs about responses. The librarian highlights words related to database structure (e.g., sort, filter, browse, keywords) and emotions students associate with databases.

LESSON OBJECTIVES STATED

Librarian Script: "Today, we are going to look at examples of databases that you might use in your everyday life and in academic situations. By the end of this lesson, you will be aware of the underlying structures and common features of databases. When you understand what they have in common, you will also recognize different search strategies that will work in most databases. This will also, hopefully, help you to be more comfortable using academic databases, and more likely to play around, explore, and discover with them."

INPUT/MODELING

The librarian explains that a database is an organized collection of data, and then shows examples of common databases, using screenshots of databases people might use in non-academic settings. Examples include Internet Movie Database (IMDB), Flickr, or retail websites.

Finally, the librarian shows a screenshot of an academic database.

The librarian points out the markers that are indicators to identify these as databases:

- Ability to sort
- Ability to limit search or filter results
- Presence of advanced search tools (the librarian may need to briefly describe these)

Each of these features implies that below the surface, this is not only a collection of data, but it is organized. There is a structure. When a searcher sorts, or limits, or combines terms in an advanced search, s/he is taking advantage of this structure to discover things and to make connections in the database.

Because of this common structure, there are many strategies and features that are the same across many databases, both academic and popular.

Examples include subject headings and the ability to limit and sort results. While these features are not related to structure, the librarian may also wish to point out that many databases use quotation marks for phrase searching and bold to highlight search terms in the list of search results.

It can be helpful to remind students that they cannot break databases; databases are to be explored. The librarian can take this opportunity to remind students that the worst thing that can happen is that they will get no results or too many results and in that case, they can just try again.

GUIDED PRACTICE/CHECK FOR UNDERSTANDING WITH INFORMAL DATABASE

The librarian instructs students to search in Flickr for photos related to their research assignments. Students spend three minutes looking for photos, then consider the following prompts about the structure of Flickr's database, which the librarian displays on a screen or whiteboard:

- Enter search term(s) in search box and go from there.
- What are the different options for sorting/ how can you sort?
- Did you filter your results?
- What options in the advanced search did you find most useful?
- What were your priorities in choosing a photo for your assignment (humor, scientific accuracy, color scheme, etc.)? How did these affect your search terms and the search options you selected?

The librarian circulates while students search, answering questions as needed. After students have searched and answered these questions, they report out on their search to the entire class. The librarian leads a discussion, emphasizing the role that the structure of the database underlying this familiar interface plays in finding documents. S/he can then transition into using the academic database.

GUIDED PRACTICE/CHECK FOR UNDERSTANDING WITH ACADEMIC DATABASE

Students will repeat the same process with an academic database. The librarian instructs students to locate scholarly articles on their research topics using an academic database. The academic database can be chosen ahead of time by the librarian and should be related to the course or research the students are doing. This is a good moment to point out that there are databases on *many* different topics, and from many different publishers.

Again, the students take three minutes to search for an article, and then turn their attention to responding to the following prompts that are displayed by the librarian:

- Enter search term(s) in search box and go from there.
- What are the different options for sorting/ how can you sort?
- Did you filter your results?
- What options in the advanced search did you find most useful?
- Consider what your priorities are in choosing an article: background information, information on a particular aspect of your topic, publication date. These will affect your search terms and which search options you select.

The librarian circulates while students search, answering questions as they arise. Students report out on their search to the entire class. Again, during this discussion, the librarian reinforces the idea of how there are common structures underlying both academic and non-academic databases.

INDEPENDENT PRACTICE

Students will conduct searches independently for their research assignment. This can be tailored to suit the needs of the assignment.

ASSESSMENT

An optional exit survey is provided as a handout.

Who Cares? Understanding the Human Production of Information

This lesson helps students understand that information is created in specific contexts with specific aims and biases and for specific needs. This lesson could also be an anticipatory set when given as an introduction to database searching.

CONCEPT IN CONTEXT

The search for information can take a variety of methods, some more strategic than others. Knowing all of the places where information might be located is difficult, if not impossible, so a practiced researcher understands that when it comes to locating information, it is the journey, not the destination, that counts. The lesson asks students to analyze one piece of information and follow the conversational thread contained within for clues to additional information on the same topic. It acknowledges the difficulty students may have in thinking about an article or information source as a piece of a larger puzzle, a voice in a greater conversation. For example, thinking about all the possible researchers or writers interested in the topic of prosthetic limbs requires students not only to consider the various disciplinary voices involved in the conversation, from engineers to marketing executives to the military, but also to think about the variety of ways those disciplines research, write, and disseminate their information.

There is considerable overlap of two threshold concepts in this lesson. Becoming a proficient searcher of information necessitates the pre-search contemplation that these input/modeling questions provoke. Students cannot begin to search for useful information until they know where to look. By assessing the topic, identifying the major "speakers," and carefully reading information found along the way, students learn the process of searching as strategic exploration, rather than a hit-or-miss grab for appropriate sources for their paper.

Overlapping Threshold Concept: This lesson also addressed the concept *Scholarship as Conversation.*

Author: Rebecca Kuglitsch, Interdisciplinary Science Librarian
University of Colorado, Boulder

Level: Intermediate. The lesson assumes students have some basic search abilities, familiarity with search engine operation, and some disciplinary knowledge.

Estimated Time: 15–30 minutes

MATERIALS NEEDED

- Students need access to a computer for guided practice exercise
- Librarian needs access to whiteboard and computer with projection system
- Optional handout *(see Appendix or www.ala.org/acrl/files/handouts.pdf)*

LEARNING GOALS

- Students will understand that information on any topic is produced by a variety of researchers, individuals, and organizations for a variety of reasons.
- Students will understand that information is disseminated in a variety of formats and venues and that this influences the search strategies they use.

ANTICIPATORY SET

The librarian engages students in a discussion, asking the following:

"What are you interested in researching? Why? Who else do you think might be interested in a similar topic? Are any aspects of the topic you have chosen to research important for creating public policy? Is your topic important to a specific industry? What would be the best way to disseminate the information you have found during your research?"

LESSON OBJECTIVE STATED

Librarian Script: "Today we are going to think about who is or might be producing and publishing (informally or formally) information about a particular topic and how this information is disseminated. Knowing who is interested in a particular topic and why can help us identify the different voices in the conversation around a topic and can help us find more information. Discovering this conversation can then help us gather a variety of viewpoints, understand the topic more fully, and draw our own conclusions."

INPUT/MODELING

The librarian can ask students for a topic, but should prepare a model topic in case no one in the class has an appropriate suggestion. Two example topics follow:

Example 1: What individuals or organizations would generate information about the use, design, distribution, and/or manufacture of prosthetic limbs?

The librarian writes student responses on the board. Possible answers may include:

- Engineers
- Government agencies
- Armed forces
- United Nations
- Orthopedic surgeons
- Rehab hospitals
- Manufacturers of prosthetic limbs
- Disabled individuals and their family members

Example 2: Who would be interested in information about the effects of parental incarceration on young children?

The librarian writes student responses on the board. Possible answers may include:

- Criminal justice practitioners
- Lawyers/judges
- Legislators
- Social workers
- Teachers/professors
- Psychologists

Regardless of the topic used, the librarian asks students why these information producers are invested in this topic, and why they are producing information. The librarian then asks students how and where each group they identified would disseminate the information they produced on this topic.

Possible answers may include:
- Websites
- Government publications
- Journals
- Newspapers
- Trade magazines
- Podcasts

GUIDED PRACTICE

Students (in groups or as individuals) take ten minutes to find an article on the topic using one of the following methods:
- Google news search
- Database (determined by librarian; ideally this will include academic and trade publications)
- .gov websites
- .org websites

Students then read or skim their article and answer the following questions:
- Describe the voice of the article/piece you found. Who is speaking, and why?
- How could the piece you found lead you to other articles or information?
- How might information produced by one group/individual influence the work of others? What evidence of this do you see in the piece you found?
- Which disciplinary perspectives are represented in your piece?

The librarian gathers the class together to share what they found and discuss any questions that they are unsure of. The intent is to address each question, and to involve as many participants as possible.

INDEPENDENT PRACTICE

Each group could be asked to find a source of information on their own topic. They must identify the person or group who wrote or disseminated this piece of information. As before, the librarian asks students to consider the following questions:

- The voices in the topic of scholarly conversation; i.e., who is speaking? Why?
- Through what disciplinary lenses are people viewing this topic? Which disciplinary information sources (like databases) would contain information about it?
- Are there other threads of conversation identifiable in this piece? Do they lead to other topics or ideas?
- What kinds of information might the U.S. government collect and provide on this topic?

ASSESSMENT

Students can be asked to write a minute paper.

Password: Keyword Edition

This game, modeled after the game Password, is used as the icebreaker at the beginning of an information literacy session. This quick, interactive lesson opens the students up to learning and thinking like a researcher.

CONCEPT IN CONTEXT

This game sets a stage for the idea that there is no one right way to think of a topic or idea. The librarian drives this idea home, then urges students to think about the way that a discipline (and the disciplinary databases that students use as tools) might use a language and vocabulary that are specific to that discipline. Searching, then, can be an exercise in experimenting with and learning about those vocabularies. This inquiry-fueled process of discovery requires inventiveness when an information seeker is setting out to find the threads of thought that weave together to make a body of knowledge about a topic. During "Password: Keyword Edition," students generate alternative words and synonyms. The intent of the exercise is to broaden their ideas about the topic and thus expand their approach to the topic, allowing for discoveries that may be unexpected and surprising. As novices, students may not realize that language even matters when using the interfaces of databases. Raising their awareness and honing their skills at experimentation can transform them as searchers and expand their capability to view searching, truly, as exploration.

Author: Melissa Langridge, User Education Coordinator
Niagara University, Lewiston, New York

Level: Basic
Estimated Time: 15–20 minutes

MATERIALS NEEDED

- Presentation technology, such as Prezi™ or PowerPoint™, used to supply keywords
- Participation incentive, e.g., candy

LEARNING GOALS

- Students will recognize that there are many different ways to talk about or refer to the same concepts.
- Students will understand that the use of different keywords results in different outcomes in databases.

ANTICIPATORY SET

This lesson itself may serve as an anticipatory set for a longer lesson on searching.

LESSON OBJECTIVE STATED

Librarian Script: "One big inhibitor in student research is not 'getting' the language of the discipline, since you haven't really been exposed to it before. Today we're going to think about words and synonyms, how they may be discipline-related, and how we need to consider them to find information."

INPUT/MODELING

The librarian provides instruction on how to play. One student will sit in the "hot seat" facing the rest of the class. A word will appear on the screen behind her or him, out of her or his field of vision. It is the goal of the rest of the class to get that individual to say the word on the screen. To do that, the students facing the screen will shout out one-word synonyms or antonyms of the word projected in order to get the student in the "hot seat" to guess the word listed. The librarian reminds students that this is not charades. The use of "sounds like" or using actions as clues is not permitted.

To further clarify these directions, either the librarian or the course instructor may come up to the front of the class to demonstrate using an example of a word that is related to the course in some way. Alternatively, a current topic from the news or an example from popular culture is a fun way to get the students engaged. Having the professor model gameplay first encourages participation. If the students are not willing to come up to play after the example, the librarian can simply offer a small incentive.

GUIDED PRACTICE

Students work as one large group generating various keywords that might be used in a database. The words that are displayed throughout the game are chosen ahead of time by the librarian, and they should be related to the course or possible research topics. A variety of words are recommended. Using a thesaurus or a textbook in the discipline may be a helpful tool for mining for words for the librarian. As the student guesses at words from the hot seat, the librarian can record the words that are the prompts and that are guesses. This list will ultimately be a list of words that someone could use as keywords in a database search. Once the word is guessed, the class takes a few minutes to brainstorm any alternative keywords. The librarian can lead a short discussion on why some words might be better than others for research.

INDEPENDENT PRACTICE

Upon completion of the game, the librarian provides a demonstration of a course-related or disciplinary database. In doing so, s/he can experiment with some of the words generated during the game, reinforcing that the various words result in different research outcomes. Optionally, the librarian could model using the thesaurus or subject term search function of a relevant database. After the database demonstration, students will have time to practice the skills they learned throughout the session when finding information on their own topics. The librarian is available to help students individually.

Approaching Problems like a Professional

In this business-specific lesson, students participate in a scenario-based learning exercise in which they discuss and synthesize information from different sources to meet an information need. The lesson is designed to teach students that, in business disciplines, research cannot be conducted in just one place, and there are many types of reliable information sources that can provide primary and secondary research. The idea for this lesson is adaptable to other disciplines, as long as the librarian uses a realistic example that students might encounter as professionals.

CONCEPT IN CONTEXT

This exploratory, real-world, practice-based lesson is designed to teach students in an upper level course about the need to find information from a variety of sources. Often, students believe (and hope) that all the information they need is accessible from a single source. This is unlikely in business (and many other disciplines) because information can be gleaned from proprietary databases, government sites, newspapers, and more.

Asking students to approach the information need like a practicing professional prompts them to think critically in order to solve a problem, rather than simply to fulfill the requirements of an assignment. Thinking like a professional underscores the need to go beyond "one-stop" researching and instead to delve into the wide variety of information sources and really explore as they discover ideas, facts, and approaches from different sources. This type of lesson has the added benefit of preparing students for information-seeking situations they may face when in the workplace.

Author: Melissa Mallon, Coordinator of Library Instruction
Wichita State University Libraries, Wichita, Kansas

Level: Intermediate to advanced

Estimated Time: 30 minutes for the scenario activity; 15 minutes for a discussion of business databases

MATERIALS NEEDED

- Whiteboard or projector and computer for the librarian

- A paper handout should include the scenario and the two questions *(see Appendix or www.ala.org/acrl/files/handouts.pdf)*

LEARNING GOALS

- Students will recognize the need to access information from a variety of sources in order to gather evidence to solve a marketing problem.
- Students will assess data retrieved from different databases in order to determine if they have enough information to complete a case analysis.

ANTICIPATORY SET

Librarian Script: "When you're looking for information about a company, or a company's marketing plan, you need to start somewhere. What kind of information might you look for? How would you go about analyzing a marketing problem to offer solutions based on real data?"

LESSON OBJECTIVE STATED

Librarian Script: "In today's class, we are going to talk about finding and using primary and secondary data to address a problem encountered by a business. This information can be provided by marketers, business professionals, etc. and can be used by businesses in a variety of scenarios."

INPUT/MODELING

The librarian asks students to work in groups to read the following case-study scenario mimicking a real-life problem in their field of study:

> You are a marketing manager for Whole Foods Market. You've just received word that tomatoes from one of your suppliers might be infected by salmonella. You are asked to provide the company with a report that details how this might affect the company both socially and financially. You remember that this has happened before—a few years ago, the spinach supply was also infected by salmonella. You decide to investigate what happened to the company during this time and if there were

any repercussions regarding consumer relations. Work in small groups to answer the following questions.

1. What do you need to know?
2. Where can you locate the information you need?

The librarian can give students time to think on their own, then give them time to discuss in small groups, or s/he can ask students to immediately begin discussing in small groups.

GUIDED PRACTICE

After the students have had time to answer these questions in groups and discuss their answers, the librarian facilitates a large group discussion with the entire class. The librarian can then ask the following questions to check their understanding and develop the idea that the search process is complex and iterative, and that it can be used to understand their discipline:

- Do you think the outbreak had any financial repercussions? How could you find that out? (This introduces the concept of locating financial statements to identify revenue trends.)
- Would this have had any long-term effects on the company? (This introduces the concept of forecasting.)
- Were there any customer relations issues? (This introduces the need to back up their ideas or assumptions with secondary data.)

After students complete the activity and discuss the questions, the librarian can lead a discussion on discipline-specific databases and research tools.

CHECK FOR UNDERSTANDING

The main method of assessment is observation during the brainstorming exercise. The librarian can walk around the room, observing discussions among classmates. The librarian can also assess student comprehension by their responses to the scenario questions. S/he can be looking for students to offer explanations for their answers and recommend searching in a variety of different sources. The librarian can either take notes as students discuss their answers or have students turn in the handout.

Databases vs. Search Engines Game

Students compete to find articles and compare search results found in a database to results found in a popular search engine.

CONCEPT IN CONTEXT

Today's students face a knowledge environment that, on the surface, makes their academic tasks seem easy; a few clicks of the mouse, and they have more information than a student two decades earlier could have collected in a week. This ease of discovery poses its own problem. Students cope with a profusion of information by falling back on search tools that are familiar, regardless of their effectiveness or accuracy. What they need to understand is that not all search tools are equal, and different tools have different rules. While students cannot know every place to find information, they can learn to recognize the difference between databases with controlled search vocabularies and powerful search engines that cast wide nets, catching much more than is needed or helpful.

Authors: Elizabeth Martin, Head Librarian, Professional Programs
Grand Valley State University, Allendale, Michigan

Rebecca Daly, Head Librarian
Finlandia University, Hancock, Michigan

Level: Basic/general education
Estimated Time: 45–50 minutes

MATERIALS NEEDED

- Computer lab with Internet access
- Subscription database
- Handout (*See Appendix or www.ala.org/acrl/files/handouts.pdf*)
- Prizes (optional)

LEARNING GOALS

- Students will understand the need for a search vocabulary.
- Students will recognize the differences in content and quality among search tools.

- Students will learn to adjust their search strategy according to information tool/collection.

ANTICIPATORY SET

Librarian Script: "When you need information, where do you look? Have you ever considered what the best tool is for searching? Do you think you could be a more effective information searcher?"

LESSON OBJECTIVE STATED

Librarian Script: "Today we will play a game that will show you the importance of finding the right search words for finding information. In this game, you will also compare the usefulness and searchability of a database vs. a search engine like Google."

INPUT/MODELING

The librarian begins a think (3 min), pair (5 min), share (3–5 min)[1] activity. Students are instructed to come up with three synonymous terms for each main idea in the thesis statement on the worksheet handout. The librarian then demonstrates separate searches using key terms and the entire thesis statement to illustrate the difference in results.

GUIDED PRACTICE

For the game, the librarian divides the class into two teams and reviews the rest of the handout and the objective of the game—to find an appropriate source to use to support the thesis statement on the worksheet—with the class. One team is assigned an academic database appropriate to the class and one is assigned a search engine (e.g., Google or Bing). Each team member will search for an article to score a point for the team. Points will be given to sources that match according to relevance and timeliness. This activity focuses on strategic searching, not evaluation. The librarian should discuss with students the need to further evaluate the information they find. Lessons from chapter 4 can be paired with or added to this one.

Teams are given five minutes to search. For every appropriate article a team member finds, the team scores one point. The librarian keeps score by reviewing each discovery and makes sure it fits the criteria on the worksheet before awarding a point. It helps to have another librarian or instructor assist with the judging and scoring. (The authors used a scoreboard widget.) The review and scoring process gives the librarian the opportunity to review with students what an academic journal article looks like and how to identify them (see handout). To officially score a point for their team, students must reflect upon whether the article would be a good source for a research paper.

In an optional second round, groups choose their tool, database or search engine and are instructed to revise their search terms from earlier searches.

INDEPENDENT PRACTICE

Students can continue to acquire points by finding other journal articles relating to the thesis statement and search criteria on the worksheet. Students only need to write down and reflect on their first approved article, but they must have a librarian review additional findings to gain points. An article cannot be used by more than one student on a team.

NOTES:

1. Frank Lyman, Jr., "The Development of Tools," *Maryland ATE Journal* 1 (1981): 20–21.

Keywording

This is an introductory lesson where students learn how to develop keywords and phrases to search for information. It works well for students who need to develop a search strategy for a broad research topic and assumes that the students come to the class with a topic already in mind.

CONCEPT IN CONTEXT

Novice researchers often are overwhelmed at the beginning of a research project and have difficulty formulating a search topic, much less a search strategy. As librarians, we know that first attempts at searching are not always fruitful, particularly when students jump into research with little thought or preparation. This simple truth can be a serious roadblock to inexperienced researchers, who may become frustrated with their lack of success or select unsuitable material due to the overwhelming number of hits they get when searching databases using broad or inappropriate keywords. This basic lesson uses a short video to encourage inquiry about a relevant topic, inspiring students to develop questions that lead to discovery. It also introduces students to the concept of strategic exploration by showing them how to develop relevant keywords and phrases before they begin their research.

Author: Cate Calhoun Oravet, Reference and Instruction
Librarian
Auburn University, Auburn, Alabama

Level: Basic/general education
Estimated Time: 50 minutes

MATERIALS NEEDED
- Computers with database access
- Keywording handout[1] (*see Appendix or www.ala.org/acrl/files/ handouts.pdf*)

LEARNING GOALS
- Students will learn how to extract relevant keywords from their research question.

- Students will be able to take these keywords and generate related words or terms that they can use to develop a search strategy.
- Students will learn how to search a library database using the keywords and terms they generated to find manageable, relevant search results.

ANTICIPATORY SET

The librarian begins class by showing a brief DVD or online video about a topic relevant to the class being taught. For example, in an environmental education class where students are studying sustainability, the students might view a short educational video about wind farms.

After viewing the video as a class, the librarian asks the class if they can think of anything they would like to know more about based on what they saw in the video (e.g., can they think of any research question that the video posed?). The librarian writes these questions on the board. Examples relating to this video might include:

- What effect do wind farms have on migrating bird populations?
- How effective are wind farms at generating energy?
- Do wind farms cut energy costs to consumers?

LESSON OBJECTIVE STATED

Librarian Script: "Today we, as a class, are going to come up with keywords and phrases that will help us search for information in order to answer this research question. After we're done, you will be able to use this technique to develop keywords and phrases to help you find information for the topic or research question that you have already developed for your paper in this class."

INPUT/MODELING

The librarian will then lead a whole class discussion/exercise based on one of these questions. For example, "What effect do wind farms have on migrating bird populations?"

The librarian projects a copy of the keywording handout on the board, or prior to class, draws a representation of the handout on the board. The librarian then introduces/states the lesson objective to the class.

1. My Topic Proposal:

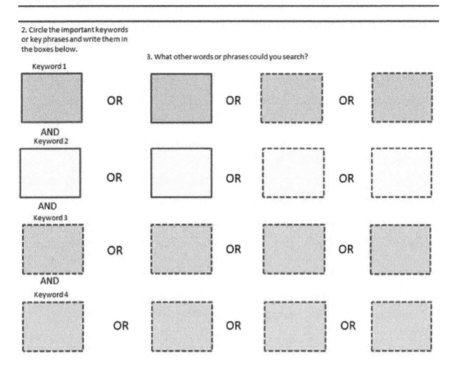

2. Circle the important keywords or key phrases and write them in the boxes below.

3. What other words or phrases could you search?

Keyword 1

AND
Keyword 2

AND
Keyword 3

AND
Keyword 4

The librarian then asks the class to identify keywords or terms that they believe will lead to information in a database that will help them answer this question. The class will work as a group to fill out a handout that is projected on the screen or written on the board. The librarian can fill out the handout or ask for a student volunteer. Primary keywords are identified as well as related terms and phrases. During this exercise the librarian makes sure that that the students are familiar with the search connectors "and" and "or" and how they affect searching in databases.

Once keywords and phrases are identified, the librarian will access a database likely to have information on the subject being researched (or ask students what they think would be an appropriate database) and project the database on the screen. Using keywords from the handout, the librarian (or a student volunteer) performs searches, demonstrates narrowing techniques, etc., and analyzes the results with the class.

GUIDED PRACTICE

The librarian instructs students to perform this same exercise in relation to the research topic they have chosen for the class. The librarian passes out copies of the handout and instructs the students to generate keywords about their chosen research topic. They are asked to fill in the solid line boxes at minimum and the dotted line boxes if they can. They are asked to access an appropriate database through their library interface and search for information about their topic using search terms and combinations they generated using their handout.

CHECK FOR UNDERSTANDING

The librarian roves the classroom or lab addressing questions and monitoring search progress.

NOTES

1. This handout example mirrors the interface of EBSCO databases. The layout can be modified to correspond with the interface of other database structures.

Framing a Topic for Library Research

In this lesson, students learn to use the ideas of audience and discipline to generate new search terms for research topics. Learning to approach topics from viewpoints other than their own can help students achieve a more nuanced and full understanding of topics.

CONCEPT IN CONTEXT

The search for information, when done well, is very rarely a one-step, linear process with a clear, intuitive path. However, inexperienced searchers may think of the search as a single act with a single tool. They may overly rely on the same processes, sources, and finding aids they have used in the past, using only the language that initially occurs to them. This leads to limited information and viewpoints. To find a rich, inclusive pool of knowledge from which to draw, students need to learn to embrace flexibility and creativity, and to vary their approach. This lesson teaches students to examine a topic they have already chosen from different angles, using a variety of search terms and relying on their peers as sounding boards in order to expand their viewpoints to allow for new discovery. It incorporates multiple searches so that students can build on what they find and realize that searches filled with discovery are also rich, messy, and iterative.

Authors: Melissa Browne, Instruction and Reference Librarian
University of California, Davis

Caitlin Plovnick, First-Year Instruction and Outreach Librarian
Sonoma State University, Rohnert Park, California

Cathy Palmer, Education and Outreach Department Head
University of California, Irvine

Richard Caldwell, Head of Library Instruction
University of California, Santa Barbara

Level: Intermediate to advanced
Estimated Time: 45 minutes

MATERIALS NEEDED
- Whiteboard or computer/overhead projector
- Handouts or access to online documents (Such as a Google Form) *(see Appendix or www.ala.org/acrl/files/handouts.pdf)*

LEARNING GOALS
- Students will recognize the importance of terminology in searching for information and will be able to generate additional terms related to their research question in order to construct effective searches.
- Students will understand that the questions of focus, purpose, and intended audience they consider in framing their own topics also impact how information is organized and where it can be found.
- Students will be able to situate their research topic within an appropriate disciplinary context in order to identify relevant search tools.
- Students will be able to describe the types of information that might be helpful in order to answer their research question for their intended audience.

ANTICIPATORY SET
Librarian Script: "If you need to search for information on a topic for a research paper, how do you come up with terms and decide where to search? What do you find most challenging about searching for information on a paper topic?"

LESSON OBJECTIVE STATED
Librarian Script: "Let's build on strategies you already use and address some of the challenges you identified. We'll consider ways to frame a topic with keywords and different disciplinary approaches to focus your research."

INPUT/MODELING

PART 1

Librarian Script: "Being thoughtful about search terms matters. If you search using the word 'cinema' and a scholar writes about 'film,' you're not likely to find that scholar's work. As you search, be on the lookout for different words that you can use to address your topic."

The librarian presents a sample topic on a slide/whiteboard that students are likely to be familiar with, e.g. flu, and asks the class to think of related words and concepts. The librarian types or writes down student suggestions. Then the librarian presents a more complex topic that has been drawn from a recent course reading along with alternate words for each facet of the topic. For example, a question to investigate may be, "Is the role of the drug industry in the medical practice unethical?"

The librarian guides the class as a group through identifying each of the key concepts, then generating lists of related terms. In this example, the key concepts and related terms would be *drug industry* (related terms: *pharmaceutical industry*, specific companies like *Lilly, GSK, Pfizer, Merck*), *medical practices* (related terms: *medicine, physicians, doctors, medical students, medical research scientists, patients, FDA*), and *medical ethics* (related terms: *conflict of interest, special interests, research funding, objectivity, clinical trials*).

PART 2

Librarian Script: "In many cases, you can examine a research question through different disciplinary lenses. This is important to consider for several reasons:
- It impacts how you describe your topic.
- It determines the tools you'll use to search for sources.
- It determines the kinds of research that are done on a topic. Business research on the drug industry approaches the topic in a very different way than medical research does."

The librarian asks students to think of some subject disciplines or scholarly communities who might be especially interested in studying this topic. The librarian types or writes down student suggestions, e.g. medicine, sociology, business.

GUIDED PRACTICE

Next, the students do a similar activity with their own topics. Students fill out a handout or create a Word/Google document to address the following prompts:

- What is your research question?
- List as many additional terms/concepts to describe your question as you can.
- Which subject discipline(s) are likely to have an interest in this question?
- Are there terms you identified which you think might fit especially well with the subject disciplines you listed?

After approximately five minutes, students swap handouts or switch seats with a classmate and add terms, questions, or suggestions to their classmate's file. Students will use their responses to help them begin to identify relevant search tools and search for sources on their topics.

INDEPENDENT PRACTICE

In-class activity or homework:
Using the files created in the previous activity, students must find two or three sources related to their topic. Students search for their own topic (or their partner's topic) and fill out a worksheet with basic citation information for each item plus answer several questions:

- What different types of sources did you find?
- Which databases or search tools did you use to find your sources?
- What audience/discipline is each source intended for?
- What different terms does each source use for your topic? Are there any that weren't in your original list?

This worksheet can be collected to determine where students are in their understanding of the lesson's learning objectives. It should also help them to focus on the purpose of their own research and give them information they need for their bibliographies.

Systems of Organization

Students create an organizational system for a set of shapes. Doing so helps them understand the purpose and process of organizing information and, in turn, better understand strategies for information retrieval.

CONCEPT IN CONTEXT

Searching as Strategic Exploration as a threshold concept encompasses a range of ideas, from the initial process of inquiry, through the process of search–learn–revise–search–again, to an understanding of information resources and their tools for storage and retrieval. Experienced searchers understand that locating the information they seek is a mix of strategy and serendipity, and they know to use what they find to find more and to learn from their mistakes. They also understand that when it comes to searching like a librarian, one uses the best tools to search the best resource for the information need. This lesson builds students' basic understanding of how information is often organized for systematic retrieval. Knowing the organizational scheme will help them retrieve information. Like other lessons in this chapter, this one does not tackle the threshold concept in its entirety, but rather focuses on one part.

Authors: Pete Ramsey, Reference and Instruction Librarian

Stephen "Mike" Kiel, Reference and Instruction Librarian
University of Baltimore, Maryland

Level: Basic
Estimated Time: 30–50 minutes

MATERIALS NEEDED

- Sets of shapes for groups (pre-cut)
- Access to computers
- Example Shapes handout (*see Appendix or www.ala.org/acrl/ files/handouts.pdf*)

LEARNING GOALS

- Students will recognize the strengths and weaknesses inherent in all organizational schemes.
- Students will understand the concepts of metadata and controlled vocabulary.
- Students will identify examples of metadata and controlled vocabulary.
- Students will use metadata and controlled vocabulary to search for research materials.

ANTICIPATORY SET

The librarian engages students in a brief discussion of organization systems using a few leading questions: "What kinds of things do you organize? How?" During the discussion, several existing systems are mentioned, among them library-specific systems (e.g. the Library of Congress classification system) and systems common to students' everyday experiences (e.g. contacts list on a phone, social media). The librarian can prompt students to think about the organization of information: "How do libraries organize information? What is a database? How does a database organize articles?"

LESSON OBJECTIVES STATED

Librarian Script: "Today you will be doing an activity to show you how things can be organized in different ways. Once you learn this concept, you can adjust your approach to finding research materials."

INPUT/MODELING

Students are organized into teams. Each group receives a set of various shapes (*See Appendix or www.ala.org/acrl/files/handouts.pdf*). They are given 5 to 10 minutes to organize the shapes into groups or categories, with the following restrictions:

- No group/category can contain only one item.
- No group/category can be "miscellaneous."
- The team should reach consensus.
- They must be able to explain their groups/categories to the class.

CHECK FOR UNDERSTANDING/GUIDED PRACTICE

Teams present their organization systems to the class. The librarian has the option of highlighting certain elements on the board. Next, students are asked how they would retrieve something in another team's system. They are encouraged to discuss the validity of systems different from their own, while recognizing that none of the systems are perfect.

After the activity, presentation, and discussion, the librarian introduces the concepts of metadata (information *about* a source) and controlled vocabulary. The librarians emphasize that most library catalogs, search engines, and databases prioritize metadata and controlled vocabulary when ranking search results.

Students are given a search task (finding a book, journal article, or other research material) in which they must use metadata elements and/or controlled vocabulary in their search strategy. Next, a short debrief is used to review how the concepts of metadata and controlled vocabulary apply to searching.

Formative assessment is used during the task to determine how well students understand the concepts. Their presentation of categories will assess how well they can translate ideas of organization into applied skills.

Chapter 6

Information Has Value

THERE ARE BOTH legal and ethical aspects to the threshold concept *Information Has Value*. These are manifested in the form of intellectual property laws and in the social contract regarding the ethical use of information. These aspects often overlap and can be very confusing to students, since information can be valued in different ways by different people.

Intellectual property laws allow the creator or owner of some information to control its use. Students seem to be aware of the existence of copyright laws, but they may not be aware that the founders of the United States believed encouraging the development and dissemination of new information was important enough to codify it in the Constitution. The United States copyright law is the promise to the creator of information that the government will acknowledge her or his right to profit from this information, provided s/he gives it to the public after a specified period of time.

Some information has economic value—someone owns it and can profit from it. The control and/or restriction of access to some information can be a new concept to students. With seemingly endless access to free information in a variety of formats, students may not realize there is a lot of information they cannot get for free. Information locked behind paywalls comes at a cost because someone profits from its distribution. Information is a commodity being produced, packaged, and distributed, just like wheat or oil. When students understand this, they can realize the value attached to some information over other information, as well as the consequences of its misuse or misattribution.

Students may not value the information they themselves produce and post freely on the Internet. They may not even think of themselves as information creators and thus be unaware that someone may be profiting from the information they create. This failure to value their own intellectual property (or even recognize they have any) often leads to the disregard of the intellectual property rights of others.

Further, some students simply reject the social contract that is the basis for both intellectual property laws and the academic and journalistic convention of acknowledging the contributions of others. They share copyrighted material knowing that they are depriving the creator of the profits and credit for her or his intellectual work.

Ethical uses of information can be difficult for students to comprehend as well. Beginning with their first class in college, students are admonished by their professors and librarians to avoid committing plagiarism. When asked why plagiarism is prohibited, students can usually recite the "give credit where credit is due" mantra. However, they frequently do not actually know how to give proper credit, and more importantly, do not know *why* this credit must be given. Based on the results of a 2006 study of student attitudes on plagiarism, Lori G. Power found that "although most students can define plagiarism acceptably, 'taking someone else's words or ideas and using them as one's own,' they have only a superficial understanding of what that means and a (sic) therefore a difficult time applying that definition in real situations."[1] She also found that they knowingly plagiarized for many different reasons including the ease in doing so, the belief that an assignment is just busywork, or pressure to get a good grade.[2] Thus, students may plagiarize the work of others without realizing they are doing so, or without caring that they do, or because they believe that if something is in the public domain, they do not have to acknowledge authorship.

Lessons in this chapter were designed to help students understand the overarching concept that information has value. By giving credit to the original ideas of others and knowing the reasons for doing so, students acknowledge the intellectual effort of the creator of the information cited. As a result, they themselves become responsible, ethical users and creators of information.

Students are told not to plagiarize, but they less often are asked to examine concrete examples of plagiarism or learn what the consequences are outside of a university setting. Patricia Bravender and Gayle Schaub give students an opportunity to examine a real-world example of plagiarism, including the repercussions that followed it. In this lesson, students learn how information producers can use their work for reputational gain and, conversely, how using others' work without attribution can damage one's own reputation. Bravender's lesson on plagiarism and copyright is meant to introduce students to these two concepts by asking students to consider their own intellectual property and the value they place on it. Even though some students do not fully acknowledge the intellectual property rights of others, these same students can be surprisingly proprietorial about their own intellectual output. Introducing students to the concept of ownership of intellectual property through their own creative work can help them understand why most people feel ownership in their creative work and why the work of others should be acknowledged. They also are asked to consider their own online presence and how others might profit from it.

Smita Avasthi, like Bravender, engages students in a discussion of various plagiarism scenarios similar to ones they may encounter in college. By examining and discussing these scenarios with their classmates, students have the opportunity to delve into the ethical issues surrounding these occurrences by determining whether, in fact, plagiarism has actually occurred.

Proper attribution and citation are essential in avoiding plagiarism and Debbie Morrow's lesson takes this idea beyond the traditional written paper. By focusing on the ubiquitous PowerPoint and Prezi presentations that students are required to prepare and deliver, Morrow's lesson shows students that intellectual property rights and the need to properly cite sources extends to not only the written word but also to visual media and images. McClure and Toth address this same issue with regard to infographics, a growing form of communication that students are likely to encounter through their academic and personal research. No matter in what format information is presented, be it in print or online, or expressed in art or music, the contributions of others must be acknowledged.

In their lesson, Rebecca Bliquez and Jane Van Galen introduce students to the Creative Commons, a place where students can not only find creative work that they can use, but where they can also make their own creative work available for others. Through this lesson, students learn about the open access model and the idea that they can be part of the information ecosystem by making their own creations available for others to use and build upon.

All of these lessons have been designed to teach students the "why" behind the threshold concept of *Information Has Value* by giving them a better understanding of their economic and ethical responsibilities as both consumers and producers of information.

NOTES

1. Lori G. Power, "University Students' Perceptions of Plagiarism," *The Journal of Higher Education* 80, no. 6 (2009): 643–662, 650.
2. Ibid., 649.

Gray Areas in Plagiarism Cases

This exercise asks students to analyze different cases of plagiarism and assess various strategies for coping with incidents of plagiarism that are less blatant than copying and pasting.

CONCEPT IN CONTEXT

The value of information is not always apparent to students. Information is immediately available from an ever-increasing variety of sources, making it difficult for students to recognize the cost of ensuring its reliability and accuracy. Open access is breaking down the subscription fee walls to expensive scholarly content. Much digital information is born online, and students entering college, having grown up with remixes and mash-ups, likely find the subject of intellectual property a confusing one. They may find the reasons for giving attribution as difficult to understand as the process of doing it.

This exercise engages students in situations similar to ones they are apt to encounter. The discussions will likely result in a range of opinions but will give students the opportunity to work through the ideas of intellectual property, fair use, and plagiarism in order to better understand and recognize it in their own research.

Author: Dr. Smita Avasthi, Public Services and Lead Instruction Librarian
Santa Rosa Junior College, Santa Rose, California

Level: Beginning to intermediate, suitable for a class of lower-division undergraduates.
Estimated Time: 50–60 minutes

MATERIALS NEEDED

- Copy of school's policy on plagiarism for reference.
- Situations of plagiarism, either on a handout or projected *(see Appendix or www.ala.org/acrl/files/handouts.pdf)*

LEARNING GOALS

- Students will examine various incidents of plagiarism that may be difficult to recognize.

- Students will determine whether plagiarism occurred and will identify strategies to cope with gray areas of plagiarism.

ANTICIPATORY SET

Librarian Script: "Most of you have heard about plagiarism and are aware that there are serious consequences to using information improperly. Sometimes it can be hard to judge whether information has been used improperly. It can be difficult to understand what consequences would be appropriate for these instances."

LESSON OBJECTIVE STATED

Librarian Script: "In today's class, you will consider possible situations of plagiarism and its consequences. By completing this exercise, you are more likely to avoid unintentional plagiarism when writing your own papers."

INPUT/MODELING

The librarian divides the class into groups and distributes or projects one of the following scenarios where plagiarism is either inadvertent or not so obvious.

- A student borrows a paper from a friend and copies word-for-word several paragraphs where source material is summarized and documented. When confronted by the friend, the student says that the sections she borrowed were just about cited sources, so she cannot see the problem. If you were the friend in this case, what would you do?
- A student has written a paper, and the body of it paraphrases another source. There is very little of the student's own writing in the paper, so if s/he documents the source, nearly every paragraph will be cited. A friend points this out when asked to proofread the paper. The paper is due the next morning. What should the student do?
- A student buys a paper off the Internet and is not "caught" by the teacher. This student goes on to work at a respectable newspaper. Years later, his stolen paper is discovered and publicized, and his reputation suffers from this disclosure. What should the editor of the newspaper do?

GUIDED PRACTICE

The librarian asks the student groups to report their findings, while encouraging the rest of the class to weigh in on the group's recommendations or responses. The entire class may discuss what they think would happen according to the school's policy of plagiarism in these cases. Students can then be asked to write a few reflective paragraphs on their understanding of plagiarism, which can be used for assessment. As another assessment option, students can be asked to rank each case of plagiarism, based upon its seriousness and their individual evaluations of the cases can be used to assess their understanding.

The Who, What, and Why of the Creative Commons

After a discussion of the concept of copyright, students are shown how, through the use of Creative Commons licenses, people can make their copyrighted work freely available for others to use. Students will learn how to search Creative Commons licensed content and how to understand the various license options Creative Commons offers to copyright holders.

CONCEPT IN CONTEXT

Developing a student's understanding of the value of information as intellectual property is an effective way of ensuring that s/he will properly attribute the information s/he uses in her or his own work. Online images are especially vulnerable to copyright infringement and unauthorized use, and librarians can help students understand their legal and ethical obligations with respect to the intellectual property rights of those who created and/or own these images. Students are ardent users of social media, yet they pay little attention to the possible exploitation of their work and run the risk of unintentionally exploiting or misappropriating the work of others via their online presence. As information specialists, librarians have a responsibility to show students how to differentiate between proprietary materials and open access or copyright-free materials that they find on the Internet. By understanding why some things are copyrighted and some things are not, and, more importantly, how to differentiate between them, students will become ethical and informed information users.

Author: Rebecca Bliquez, Lead Librarian for Online Research and Instruction
Seattle University, Seattle, Washington

Jane Van Galen, Professor, School of Education
University of Washington, Bothell

Level: Basic/Intermediate
Estimated Time: 60–90 minutes

MATERIALS NEEDED

- Links to videos
- Copyright basics by the Copyright Clearance Center: https://www.youtube.com/watch?v=Uiq42O6rhW4 (6 minutes)
- Creative Commons licensing: http://creativecommons.org/videos/creative-commons-kiwi (6 minutes)
- Links to library guides for copyright resources provided by your university or library if available
- Link to overview of different Creative Commons license variables/options: http://creativecommons.org/licenses//
- Access to computer lab or students can bring their own personal computers
- Handout containing links to sources of open access images (*See Appendix or www.ala.org/acrl/files/handouts.pdf*)

Optional: All of these links can be listed in a course management system such as Blackboard, or students can be asked to sign up for Diigo accounts or another tool that facilitates group sharing (e.g. class wiki, alternative bookmarking site, group space within a campus course management system, etc.).

LEARNING GOALS

- Students will be introduced to copyright and how the Creative Commons was developed to allow people to control and share their work.
- Students will learn to effectively search for, evaluate, and use Creative Commons licensed content.

ANTICIPATORY SET

Librarian Script: "Have you ever needed an image to use for a class paper or project? Where did you get it? Do you think the image you used was covered by U.S. copyright law? Did you give the owner of the image credit? Did you ask her or his permission? Do you think your use was lawful? Ethical? A lot of the images you find on the Internet are actually protected by U.S. copyright law and you are violating the law if you use them without permission."

LESSON OBJECTIVES STATED

Librarian Script: "Today we will go over the basics of copyright, important issues to consider, and how the Creative Commons was set up in response to some of these issues. By the end of our lesson, you will have the skills necessary to search for images licensed by Creative Commons and evaluate them for credibility and relevance to individual projects."

INPUT

The librarian tells the class that they will be watching a short video about copyright law. Students are advised to take notes during this video so they can discuss at its conclusion. A six-minute video created by the Copyright Clearance Center can be found at https://www.youtube.com/watch?v=Uiq42O6rhW4.

After watching the video, the librarian engages class in a discussion about what they learned including:

- What does copyright mean?
- Why do we have a copyright law?
- What can be copyrighted?
- What are the rights of the copyright holder?

The librarian then introduces the concept of Creative Commons by telling the class that there are ways to find images and content for their projects that can be used without violating anyone's copyrights.

Librarian Script: "The first way is to find images that are no longer under copyright—that is, in the public domain. Usually this happens when the copyright expires. Determining whether something is in the public domain can be very difficult, since the length of copyright has changed over the past hundred years. An easier way is to look for images that people have made available through a Creative Commons license."

The librarian tells the class that they are now going to watch another short video, this time about the Creative Commons. (Six minute video found at http://creativecommons.org/videos/creative-commons-kiwi.)

The librarian again engages the class in discussion about what they learned about Creative Commons, particularly, the different types of licenses and how they can find images. What are the advantages to using images that are licensed under a Creative Commons license? The librarian can lead a discussion about the purpose and importance of alternatives to traditional copyright.

GUIDED PRACTICE

If pertinent, the librarian can provide a demonstration of the library's online guide that provides access to various copyright-friendly resources that students could use to find Creative Commons licensed content. Alternately, the librarian can distribute a handout containing links to open access images that can be freely used or used under one of the Creative Commons licenses (see *Appendix or www.ala.org/acrl/files/handouts.pdf*).

The last part of class is reserved for group search time. Students are instructed to look for images, media, and open education content for use in their research in a collaborative setting. They are also instructed to interpret the Creative Commons license to determine their responsibility. Often, this will include attribution. This activity is designed to promote conversation and sharing of interesting finds that also worked well. Students naturally begin to work together, with more experienced individuals serving as mentors to their peers.

INDEPENDENT PRACTICE

Students are asked to identify one Creative Commons licensed object that they could use for their project. The librarian can ask for volunteers to show the class how they searched, what they found, and how they planned to use it. If a course management system or other type of group collaboration space (social bookmarking site, wiki, etc.) is being used, all students could be asked to post this information to the site and comment on what other students have found. This is an effective way to assess student learning and promote group collaboration and sharing online.

METHODS OF ASSESSMENT

- Students post copyright-friendly works related to their topic of interest to their course-collaboration space. To demonstrate understanding of the lesson, they are also required to provide a short description of the resource, search strategies used to find it, how it will frame or contribute to their project, and what is required to appropriately use/cite/modify the work. They must also describe one thing learned from their process that they think would be beneficial to the rest of the group.

- Students can create a Creative Commons license for their class project and explain why they chose the type of license that they did.

Plagiarism v. Copyright Infringement

This lesson asks students to consider their own intellectual property and how they would feel if someone took credit for or profited from something they created. Through this reflection, students come to understand the concepts of plagiarism, copyright, and the value of information in the form of intellectual property.

CONCEPT IN CONTEXT

The value of information can be realized in a number of ways. It can mean financial, social, or professional gain. When information is misappropriated, problems may arise for both the creator and the misuser. Of all the threshold concepts in information literacy, the idea of intellectual property and the responsible use of information may be the most difficult for students to grasp. They may realize that there are consequences for passing off someone's information as their own, but they may not truly understand why doing so is problematic. Beyond the legal and ethical issues surrounding the downloading of music or films, students may fail to understand the potential damage from the misuse of information in an academic or professional situation.

Without a clear understanding of copyright and plagiarism, student producers of information may unknowingly put their own academic integrity at risk. This lesson puts students in the position of information creators so that they may consider the issues of plagiarism and copyright infringement from that viewpoint.

Author: Patricia Bravender, Professional Programs Librarian
Grand Valley State University, Allendale, Michigan

Level: Intermediate
Estimated Time: 30–45 minutes

MATERIALS NEEDED

- Optional handout/prompt containing definitions of 'plagiarism' and 'copyright' and/or the proposed scenarios *(see Appendix or www.ala.org/acrl/files/handouts.pdf)*

LEARNING GOALS

- Students will understand the basic concepts of plagiarism and copyright and the difference between committing plagiarism and copyright infringement.
- Students will become aware of common misconceptions about copyright law and plagiarism.

ANTICIPATORY SET

The librarian leads a discussion with students based on the following questions:

- How many of you have worked really hard to write a paper for a class?
- How would you feel if someone simply took that paper and turned it in under their own name?
- What is it called when someone takes someone else's work and passes it off as their own? (*plagiarism*)
- What if you wrote a book and started selling it? How would you feel if someone bought a copy from you and then turned around and posted it online for anyone to read?
- What is it called when someone takes your creation and copies and/or distributes it without your permission? (*copyright infringement*)

LESSON OBJECTIVE STATED

Librarian Script: "People often get the concepts of plagiarism and copyright infringement mixed up. Essentially plagiarism is a breach of ethics or morality and copyright infringement is breaking the law. Today we are going to talk about the differences and then work together to identify examples of both."

INPUT/MODELING

Librarian Script:

Let's discuss plagiarism first. The official definition of plagiarism is:

"[t]he action or practice of taking someone else's work, idea, etc., and passing it off as one's own; literary theft."[1] Another definition is, "the act of using another person's words or ideas without giving credit to that person."[2]

Plagiarism is considered to be morally wrong but it is not illegal. There is no *law* against committing plagiarism, however, the practice can have serious consequences. It is considered to be a form of academic dishonesty and students can be kicked out of college for committing it. Academics/professors who commit plagiarism might lose their reputations or may be forced to leave academia. Plagiarism is considered to be a breach of ethics when committed by journalists and they are sometimes fired for doing it. Authors of books who commit plagiarism can seriously damage their reputations.

The librarian asks students if they can think of any examples of plagiarism that were reported in the news. If not, the librarian could introduce one or more of the following examples[3] or find a more recent example and discuss with the students the details of the plagiarism and what, if anything, happened to the offender.

- Rand Paul accused of plagiarizing Wikipedia content
- Kendra Marr of Politico accused of plagiarism of news stories
- Fareed Zakaria accused of plagiarizing New Yorker article
- Alex Haley accused of including plagiarized material in *Roots*
- Doris Kearns Goodwin accused of including plagiarized material in her book *The Fitzgeralds and the Kennedys*

Note: Performing a Google search of the author's name with or without the term "plagiarism" shows the students how the charge of plagiarism is now forever associated with that author. The librarian could also note that the charge of plagiarism follows these authors in their Wikipedia and other biographical entries.

Librarian Script:

> Now let's talk about copyright. What does it mean when someone has a copyright?
>
> **Copyright** is "The right to control the copying, distributing, performing, displaying, and adapting of *works* (including paintings, music, books, and movies). The right belongs to the creator, or persons who buy the rights from the creator. This right is created, regulated, and limited by the federal Copyright Act …and the U.S. Constitution."[4]
>
> The moment you put pen to paper or take a photo, you own the copyright to those things. You do not need to use the copyright symbol or register it with the copyright office to own a copyright. But copyright only applies to *original* works that are fixed in a *tangible medium of expression*.[5] (The librarian asks the class what that means.)
>
> When someone violates or uses another person's copyrighted material is it called *copyright infringement*.
>
> **Copyright infringement** is "The unauthorized making, using, selling, or distributing of something protected by a …copyright…"[6] Copyright infringement is enforced by the courts and is a legal issue.

The librarian can ask students if they can think of any examples of copyright infringement that were reported in the news. Recent examples include:

- Robin Thicke accused of infringing Marvin Gaye's copyright of the song "Got to Give It Up" in his song "Blurred Lines."
- Copyright dispute over the tattoo on actor Ed Helms's face in the movie *The Hangover, Part II*. Creator of the tattoo claimed it was designed specifically for boxer Mike Tyson and was subject to copyright.

The librarian should be sure to point out that it is possible to commit plagiarism and copyright infringement at the same time and ask students how that could happen. The librarian should have a few examples if the students are unable to come up with any.

GUIDED PRACTICE/CHECK FOR UNDERSTANDING

Option 1: The librarian can break students into groups/pairs and give each one of the following scenarios. After they discuss the scenario, one representative from each scenario can lead class discussion on the question. All students should have access to the scenarios used, either through a handout or screen projection.

Option 2: The librarian leads the class discussion.
On the question regarding the ethics, students will have varying viewpoints; however, the scenarios in this lesson were chosen because there is a fairly clear case to be made that these are unethical actions. The italicized text following each question below offers discussion points for the librarian.

Scenario 1
Suppose you wrote a poem and posted it on your blog. Someone you do not know wrote music to accompany your poem, and posted a video of a cat lip-synching your poem set to music on YouTube where it became a huge hit.
- Did the person who used your poem commit plagiarism or copyright infringement? *(Both)*
- Is the act ethical?
- Do you have any legal recourse? *(Ask YouTube to remove. Ask person to stop, either informally or through a lawyer. Alternately, if you like it, you can ask for authorship credit or do nothing at all.)*
- Would it be worth it to sue? *(It would depend on possible monetary damages but probably not unless the cat singing your lyrics became the jingle for a national ad campaign for Taco Bell.)*

Scenario 2

Suppose you wrote an apocalyptic vampire novel and are selling digital copies on Smashwords for $3.99. It has become a surprise best seller and you are selling hundreds of copies every week. Someone purchased a digital copy from you and then began selling print copies on the Internet through their own personal website. You are still listed as the author.

- Did this person commit plagiarism or copyright infringement? *(Copyright infringement)*
- Is the act ethical?
- Do you have any legal recourse? (*Ask them to stop. If they do not stop, you can sue.*)
- Would be worth it to sue? (*If they will not quit, you probably will want to, they are eating into your profits.*)

Scenario 3

Suppose you are an amateur photographer and have a web page where you post your best photos. One day you are in the mall and see a calendar for sale that had one of your bird photos on the cover. You are absolutely positive it is the same photo that you posted.

- Did the person who put your photo on the calendar commit plagiarism or copyright infringement? *(Both)*
- Is the act ethical?
- Do you have any legal recourse? *(Same as above)*
- Would it be worth it to sue? (*If the calendar is generating lots of profits it might be worth it.*)

NOTES

1. *Oxford English Dictionary.* http://www.oed.com, s.v. "plagiarism," Accessed November 3, 2014.
2. *Merriam Webster Dictionary*, http://www.merriam-webster.com, s.v. "plagiarism," Accessed November 3, 2014.
3. Details about these cases are widely available on the Internet.
4. Daniel Oran, *Oran's Dictionary of the Law*, 4th ed. Clifton Park, N.Y.: Thomson Delmar Learning, 2008, 123, s.v. "copyright."
5. 17 USC §102 (2011).
6. Oran, 267, s.v. "copyright infringement."

Recognizing Plagiarism

This lesson gives students an opportunity to discuss the concept of plagiarism and their opinions of the penalties imposed by their educational institution. They are then able to analyze a real world example and discuss the consequences that followed.

CONCEPT IN CONTEXT

Information has value: monetary, intellectual, social, and professional. Students may be tempted to associate the term *value* with money; however, they need to think beyond monetary terms when it comes to information's real value. It comes from the time, intellectual energy, creativity, and other resources that go into its creation. Proficient, responsible users and creators of information recognize the importance of properly attributing the sources they use in their work to recognize its value. The Internet offers up an endless amount of information, but without clear rules for attribution like the ones included in scholarly databases (and often without clear indication of authorship), it can be confusing for students to recognize or even understand the need to cite sources. It is necessary to make clear to students the rules about plagiarism within their institution. It is equally necessary to make clear to them why those rules exist. Their reputation as scholars, as originators of new ideas built on the ideas of others, rests on the careful use of information.

Authors: Patricia Bravender, Professional Programs Librarian

Gayle Schaub, Liberal Arts Librarian
Grand Valley State University, Allendale, Michigan

Level: General Education/Basic Skills
Estimated Time: 15–20 minutes

MATERIALS NEEDED

- Handouts containing article excerpts provided below, or excerpts can be projected on a screen *(see Appendix or www.ala. org/acrl/files/handouts.pdf)*

LEARNING GOALS

- Students will learn to define plagiarism; why "borrowed words" and "borrowed ideas" need to be properly acknowledged and cited.
- Students will learn the difference between quoting and summarizing and how either, if not done correctly, constitutes plagiarism.

ANTICIPATORY SET

The librarian leads a discussion with students that includes the following questions:

"On almost every class syllabus you receive there is a statement about academic integrity that includes a warning against committing plagiarism. What is plagiarism? What are the penalties at [your college or university] for committing plagiarism? Do you think they are fair?

Plagiarism is defined as the action or practice of taking someone else's work, idea, etc., and passing it off as one's own; literary theft.[1] Penalties for students who commit plagiarism in college may range from failing a specific assignment or an entire course, or even dismissal from the university."

LESSON OBJECTIVE STATED

Librarian Script: "Today we are going to look at a real world example of an accusation of plagiarism and you will be asked to determine if you think that plagiarism did occur and, if so, how the author could have avoided it."

INPUT/MODELING

Students are introduced to a passage from an article in *The New Yorker* by Jill Lepore[2] and a passage from a column in *Time Magazine* by columnist and CNN television host Fareed Zakaria.[3] This can be done prior to class or during class.

From Lepore's 4/22/2012 New Yorker article:	From Zakaria's 8/20/2012 Time Magazine column:
As Adam Winkler, a constitutional-law scholar at U.C.L.A., demonstrates in a remarkably nuanced new book, "Gunfight: The Battle Over the Right to Bear Arms in America," firearms have been regulated in the United States from the start. Laws banning the carrying of concealed weapons were passed in Kentucky and Louisiana in 1813, and other states soon followed: Indiana (1820), Tennessee and Virginia (1838), Alabama (1839), and Ohio (1859). Similar laws were passed in Texas, Florida, and Oklahoma. As the governor of Texas explained in 1893, the "mission of the concealed deadly weapon is murder. To check it is the duty of every self-respecting, law-abiding man.	Adam Winkler, a professor of constitutional law at UCLA, documents the actual history in Gunfight: The Battle over the Right to Bear Arms in America. Guns were regulated in the U.S. from the earliest years of the Republic. Laws that banned the carrying of concealed weapons were passed in Kentucky and Louisiana in 1813. Other states soon followed: Indiana in 1820, Tennessee and Virginia in 1838, Alabama in 1839 and Ohio in 1859. Similar laws were passed in Texas, Florida and Oklahoma. As the governor of Texas (Texas!) explained in 1893, the "mission of the concealed deadly weapon is murder. To check it is the duty of every self-respecting, law-abiding man."

GUIDED PRACTICE/CHECK FOR UNDERSTANDING

Students work in groups to read and discuss the two passages and answer questions; if time is short, the librarian can facilitate a whole class exercise around the following questions.

- What is the problem? Why the accusation of plagiarism?
- How could Zakaria have avoided the accusation?
- Zakaria was suspended from *Time* and CNN for a month as a penalty for committing plagiarism. Was the penalty fair? What was the effect on his reputation?

If students have access to a computer, the librarian can ask students to do a search for Zakaria and note how the plagiarism accusation has followed him. If not in a lab, the librarian can do the search and project the results on the screen.

NOTES

1. *Oxford English Dictionary.* www.oed.com, s.v. "plagiarism," Accessed November 15, 2014.
2. Jill Lepore, "One Nation, Under the Gun," *The New Yorker,* April 23, 2012, http://www.newyorker.com/reporting/2012/04/23/120423fa_fact_lepore?currentPage=all.
3. Fareed Zakaria, "The Case for Gun Control: Why Limiting Easy Access to Guns is Intelligent and American," *Time,* August 20, 2012, 17.

Louder than Words: Using Infographics to Teach the Value of Information and Authority

In this lesson, students critically evaluate infographics by considering their rhetorical purpose(s), understanding their creation processes, and investigating their transmission through social media channels. Students will also recognize the importance of citing sources and the role citation plays in increasing credibility.

CONCEPT IN CONTEXT

The threshold concept *Information Has Value* is invoked in this lesson in which infographics are defined and explored. The genre of infographics is burgeoning in the fields of business communication, health communication, advertising, and marketing. Students are likely to encounter these sources of information on a daily basis.

Using social media, anyone can easily distribute and repost information, especially in stand-alone formats like PDFs. While these distribution channels in many ways are wonderful in terms of being able to share information, the mechanisms of social media can also have the effect of divorcing information from its creator and original contexts. In other words, social media channels may rob information creators of the political, social, and economic value of their work.

Sometimes infographics can have value in a monetary sense, in that they may drive charitable donations, sales, or political support through their persuasive capability. As users and potential creators of information available in infographics, students must understand that the information used to create infographics also has value. Adequate citation of sources is essential in order to honor the value of that information.

Another element that students should be mindful of is credibility of sources, both of the infographics and the sources that are used in the creation of the infographics. This idea of credibility is closely related to the threshold concept of *Authority is Constructed and Contextual*. As information consumers, students should be careful to understand the reason behind the creation of information in any form, including infographics, so they can more fully appreciate the value of that information and how much it should be trusted. As information creators, students should recognize that their own authority and credibility is established in part by being transparent about their sources.

This lesson teaches about the issues of authority and information's value through examination and guided discussion. It was developed for a Visual Rhetoric and Document Design course but has applicability to a wide variety of courses. The librarian can choose to adapt this lesson to focus on either of the threshold concepts or to specific disciplines by choosing example infographics that relate to those disciplines.

Authors: Hazel McClure, Liaison Librarian to English, Writing, and Environmental Studies

Christopher Toth, Assistant Professor of Writing
Grand Valley State University, Allendale, Michigan

Overlapping Threshold Concept: This lesson also addresses the concept *Authority is Constructed and Contextual.*

Level: Basic to advanced

Estimated Time: 75–90 minutes

MATERIALS NEEDED

- Example infographics. Many are available in one of these online repositories: *Cool Infographics* (http://www.coolinfographics.com), *Visual.ly* (http://www.visual.ly), or *Daily Infographic* (http://www.dailyinfographic.com). The librarian should find, at a minimum, an infographic with no citations, an infographic with misinformation, and an infographic that clearly attributes credit to sources.
- Computers for students to access the infographic repositories (or three to five printed infographics for groups to share)
- Projection capabilities for the librarian.

LEARNING GOALS

- Students will see infographics as sources of information.
- Students will attribute intellectual credit to the makers of infographics and consider the responsibility of an infographic creator to give credit to her or his sources of information.
- Students will evaluate the trustworthiness of the information in selected infographics.

ANTICIPATORY SET

The librarian asks students, "Think back—when was the last time you shared a link on social media or via email? Where did that information originate? Who wrote it? Was it 'good' information?" In the brief discussion that follows, the librarian can guide students to think about these links as information that originated somewhere. To put together this document, the creator possibly did research to gather information. The librarian can share an infographic at this point, ideally one that includes data or facts and relates in some way to the discipline of the class.

LESSON OBJECTIVE STATED

Librarian Script: "Today we're going to examine some infographics and decide whether they're reliable as information sources or not. We'll also be thinking about the creation of the infographics and what is required of their creators to communicate the value of the information to an audience."

INPUT/MODELING

With the infographic from the Anticipatory Set still being displayed, the librarian provides a definition of the genre of infographics. In his definition of infographics, Christopher Toth explains:

> [Infographics] attempt to educate an audience about a specific topic or issue in a visually interesting and easily navigable manner through a combination of words and visuals. Infographics often communicate complex quantitative and/or qualitative information quickly for their audience. They typically combine data displays, lists, graphics, and other visual

elements to make a point; they intend to inform, and frequently persuade, their intended audience about a focused topic.[1]

Following this definition, the librarian points out that infographics are documents that contain information, much like many library resources with which students may already be familiar, such as book chapters, newspapers, or journal articles. The librarian asks how infographics are different from other sources of information. For instance, "How is an infographic different from a newspaper article? How is it different from a scholarly article?"

The discussion that ensues in response to these questions will ideally 1) reinforce the definition of an infographic and 2) prompt students to consider the different ways infographics are produced, shared, and read.

Some possible points to be raised are that infographics:

- Are visual. As people read, they have emotional responses to images.
- Are often data-driven. Data, like imagery, is persuasive.
- Contain a lot of information in a small space.
- Easily shared via social media platforms.

Using the idea that infographics are quite persuasive and that they are often created to convince an audience about issues and/or to act on them, the librarian will guide the conversation to the ethical imperative for infographic creators to be clear about sources of information, to be accurate, and to attribute the facts to information sources. At this point in the lesson, the librarian can turn the discussion to the need to attribute credit by citing sources.

The librarian can ask, "Why do we cite information in, say, a first-year composition research paper?" Some likely answers are:

- It is a requirement of the assignment.
- It is important to be able to find the sources of the information.
- It is necessary to give credit to the creator of the information.

What the class may not address is that citing sources builds the writer's credibility. If a student makes a claim, but doesn't provide a source for the information, the audience will question the student's credibility. It's important for the librarian to tease this point out, because the class will be thinking about the effect of infographics with no citations.

Next, the librarian displays the infographic with no citations. S/he asks the students to identify the infographic's purpose(s). The purpose might be to inform, persuade, or sell, or some combination of these. Then, s/he asks where the creators of the infographic got their information. Since the librarian has chosen an infographic without a citation, students will not know. The librarian then asks about the effect of not knowing the sources of the information presented. Most students will likely say that they no longer trust the information and question the creator's credibility.

Next, the librarian reiterates that infographics are an information source, and s/he briefly discusses some questions that are essential to understanding the authority or credibility of any source of information. [*Optional:* If the librarian would like to focus the lesson on authority s/he can spend more time on the following questions, perhaps having students work in groups to answer these questions about specific infographics.]

- What are the sources of information that are communicated? Are they clear?
- What sources are listed?
- Are the sources that are listed credible? Why or why not?
- Who's presenting the information and why?
- What financial interests are at stake?

The librarian can then present the other example infographics to discuss the ways that citations are or are not used and what affect this has on an audience.

GUIDED PRACTICE

The librarian asks students to find an infographic that appeals to them in one of the repositories listed in the "Materials Needed" section above. After giving students time to find them, the librarian posts or distributes the following list of questions as a handout:

From the infographic and the website where it appears try to answer the following questions:

- What sources are cited?

- Who is the creator/author of the infographic?
- What is the purpose of the infographic?
- Who is the intended audience?
- What financial interests are in play?

Using the Internet, try to find:
- Where did this infographic originally appear?

And choose one of the following:
- Check out one of the sources cited. Does it appear to be legitimate? How can you tell?
- Choose one claim that's included in the infographic. Try to find a different source that confirms this claim.

The librarian gives students about ten minutes to answer these questions, asking students to be ready to consider this final question: "If you were the creator of this infographic, what would you change to make it more credible?" [*Optional:* If the librarian and faculty member would like to focus on the evaluative aspect of this lesson, s/he can ask instead, "Is this infographic trustworthy? Why or why not?"] After students have considered their infographic and taken notes, the class discusses their findings as a group. As the students discuss the answers to their questions, the librarian displays the infographics being described and discussed on the projection screen and tries to have students address different questions posed on the handout.

In addition to some of the issues that have already been discussed, the following are points the librarian may want to emphasize as they come up in conversation:

- Many infographics exist to sell products, even if that's not readily apparent. Searching for sources and tracking down who wrote an infographic or where it originally appeared can reveal that the financial interests behind the infographic.
- Sometimes the citations provided are not specific (i.e., www. nytimes.com), and so aren't really useful citations.
- Sometimes the citations provided do not give appropriate credit for the information.

Social media venues sometimes conceal the source of the infographic and separate it from its original context, which obscures its purpose. In many ways, this makes it difficult for audiences to adequately evaluate the quality of information.

CHECK FOR UNDERSTANDING:

The librarian can check for understanding during class conversation or small group discussion (if group discussion is used).

NOTES

1. Christoper Toth, "Revisiting a Genre: Teaching Infographics in Business and Professional Communication Courses," *Business Communication Quarterly* 76, no. 4 (2013): 446–457, 448.

Ethical Use of Information in Presentations

Students learn the importance of attributing non-textual sources of information within the context of a presentation.

CONCEPT IN CONTEXT

Like the other lessons in the chapter, this lesson concentrates on the value of information and the need to acknowledge that value through accurate attribution of sources. Unlike the others, however, it focuses not on print sources but on images and their use within the context of a presentation instead of a written paper. An effective presentation uses images that enhance the message rather than slides filled with bullet-pointed text. For students, finding the right image can be tricky. Ascertaining whether or not that image can be freely used and, more importantly, why or why not, can be even trickier. By taking students through librarian-created slides featuring a variety of images appropriately used and attributed, the lesson gets to the heart of the issue of information's value, as intellectual property, as a measure of one's reputation, and as a tool for scholarly or professional gain. Students discuss and, hopefully, develop an understanding of what goes into the creation of information in the form of an image and why that creative and intellectual effort deserves the respect and attribution of others who use it to create new information.

Overlapping Threshold Concept: This lesson also addresses the concept *Authority is Constructed and Contextual.*

Author: Debbie Morrow, Liaison Librarian
Grand Valley State University, Allendale, Michigan

Level: Basic/general education
Estimated Time: 30 minutes

MATERIALS NEEDED

- PC/projector/screen are required; Internet is desirable.

LEARNING OBJECTIVES

- Students will learn that copyright and intellectual property rights extend beyond words and texts to visual media and the use of images in presentation slides.
- Students learn why it is important to attribute the sources they use in their research, regardless of format.

ANTICIPATORY SET

Librarian Script: "At some time in school you will probably have to do a presentation. If you've given a presentation, or watched a presentation, you realize the importance of keeping the audience interested while at the same time letting the audience know it is hearing from an informed, credible speaker."

LESSON OBJECTIVE STATED

Librarian Script: "Today we're going to review a concept you are already somewhat familiar with—crediting sources of words and ideas that are not your own—and extend it to other kinds of intellectual property and other types of delivery besides written research papers. Giving credit to the creators of the information you use makes your process transparent and, therefore, makes you a credible researcher and presenter."

INPUT/MODELING

Students are led by the librarian through a set of presentation slides designed to model preparing a presentation that includes images. Associated with each slide are questions that provoke thought and discussion about why students should cite the source of their information, in whatever format it exists.

The following slides are to be created by the librarian, using images described in the mockups, as appropriate for the class.

In Slide 1, students are encouraged to let a picture be worth a thousand words. Thoughtful use of visuals, including images in a presentation, can give audience members a clear idea of a message. The librarian posts an image or images obviously created by someone else. Students are challenged to consider whether the producer(s) of the image(s) should be credited for the same reasons that authors of books and articles are quoted and referenced.

Slide 1:

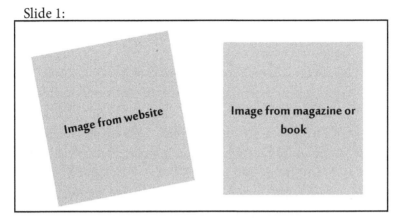

- Whose images are these?
- Where did they come from?
- How do you know?
- Why does it matter?
- May you use them freely for any purpose whatsoever?

The librarian discusses the questions listed in bullet points above with the class. The librarian can introduce the concept of fair use. For a classroom presentation, students do not infringe on the rights of copyright holders when using their images. As soon as a presentation goes anywhere beyond a one-time in-class showing, there is an obligation to obtain permission for the intended use from each rights holder. Sometimes, getting permission can be difficult, if not impossible.

Slide 2 allows students to discuss options for finding visual information elsewhere.

Slide 2:

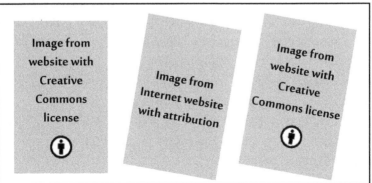

- Sites like CC Search, flickr.com, morguefile.com, imagebase.net, wylio.com, and Google offer images tagged with Creative Commons licenses.
- Sometimes, though, you still can't find what you need. Consider creating your own image, or use what you can find, but give credit to the creator.

Slide 3 illustrates a situation in which a photograph is used as part of a presentation. It wouldn't be obvious to a presentation viewer whether this photo is or isn't from a source like Flickr.com, but matching the in-line citation to full references or credits would reveal that the rights holder also happens to be the author of the slide presentation.

Slide 3:

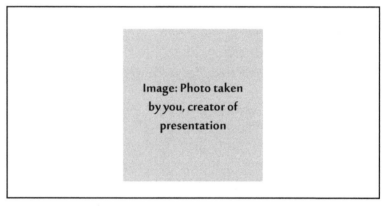

- What if you use your own photograph(s) to illustrate parts of your presentation?
- Should you credit yourself?
- Why? Why not?

The librarian facilitates discussion about why a credit should follow every image in a presentation, based on the questions following each slide, making sure to include the following:

Intellectual property: Thought and energy went into creating any image. Ethical researchers honor someone else's work.

Credibility and authority: Images provide evidence for one's statements. Images without credit undermine the credibility of the message and the authority of the presenter.

Plagiarism: Student scholars can guarantee the accuracy of their work and the soundness of their research by making sure the images in a paper or presentation are properly attributed.

Protection of one's own work: Student scholars are creators of new information. When their information is shared outside the classroom, either online or in-person, students' own images and information become vulnerable to unattributed reuse or exploitation.

Finally, Slide 4 provides image credits. It is suggested that the credits may be formatted following principles of whichever style manual has been selected, but in a presentation, it may be helpful to separate them from a list of "Sources Cited," and group them in an "Image Credits" section by slide numbers or captions.

Slide 4:

Image Credits
Credit 1 (from Slide 1)
Credit 2 (from Slide 1)
Credit 3 (from Slide 2)
Credit 4 (from Slide 2)
Credit 5 (from Slide 2)
Credit 6 (from Slide 3)

- Librarian adds credits from images in slides 1–3 here, according to the format used in the class.
- The emphasis is the reason *why* we cite, not *how*. It is less important to cover the mechanics of citation.

Like the credits that roll at the end of a feature film, the image credit slide is necessary, even though the audience rarely reads it. The librarian can lead a brief discussion about format or style, making sure to address the true purpose of this portion of a presentation.

Lessons with Overlapping Information Literacy Threshold Concepts

SOME LESSONS IN this collection address more than one information literacy threshold concept. Users of this book who are looking for ideas to teach specific threshold concepts may want to also consider the following lessons listed below under the additional concept each addresses.

SCHOLARSHIP AS CONVERSATION
- Context through Citation by *Jenny Fielding*
- Who Cares? Understanding the Human Production of Information by *Rebecca Kuglitsch*

RESEARCH AS INQUIRY
- Mapping Scholarly Conversation by *Kathleen Anne Langan*

INFORMATION CREATION AS A PROCESS
- Non-Scholarly Formats as Research Tools by *Rachel M. Minkin*
- Crafting a Credible Message by *Debbie Morrow*

AUTHORITY IS CONSTRUCTED AND CONTEXTUAL

- Using Sources to Support a Claim by *Dani Brecher*
- Tracing Information over Time by *Xan Goodman*
- Ethical Use of Information in Presentations by *Debbie Morrow*
- Louder than Words: Using Infographics to Teach the Value of Information and Authority by *Hazel McClure & Christopher Toth*
- Starting Points: The Role of Blogs in Scholarly Conversation by *Brandon West*

SEARCHING AS STRATEGIC EXPLORATION

- Using Information as a Springboard to Research by *Emily Frigo & Jessalyn Richter*
- Crafting a Credible Message by *Debbie Morrow*
- Starting Points: The Role of Blogs in Scholarly Conversation by *Brandon West*

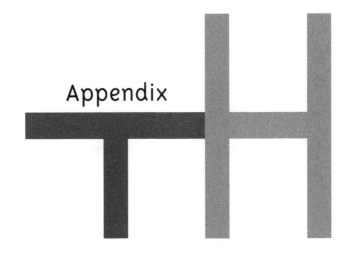

Lesson Handouts

Also available online at www.ala.org/acrl/files/handouts.pdf.

CHAPTER 1
The Conversational Nature of Sources of Information

ANDREA BAER

Citations to assigned sources:

Taibbi, Matt. "Ripping Off Young America: The College-Loan Scandal."
    Rolling Stone, August 15, 2013. http://www.rollingstone.com/politics/
    news/ripping-off-young-america-the-college-loan-scandal-20130815

Richwine, Jason. "What 'Profits'? Rolling Stone's Matt Taibbi
    Misunderstands Student Loans." *National Review Online*, August
    23, 2013. http://www.nationalreview.com/corner/356551/what-
    profits-rolling-stones-matt-taibbi-misunderstands-student-loans-
    jason-richwine

For the Taibbi article, identify:

1. the publication source, as well as the publication's general audi-
    ence and purpose

2. the source's general purpose (e.g., to inform, to make an argument)
3. the source's central message or argument
4. one or two pieces of supporting evidence used to convey the central message or argument

For the Richwine article, identify:
1. the publication source, as well as the publication's general audience and purpose
2. the source's general purpose (e.g., to inform, to make an argument)
3. the source's central message or argument
4. one or two pieces of supporting evidence used to convey the central message or argument

CHAPTER 1
Using Information as a Springboard to Research

EMILY FRIGO & JESSALYN RICHTER

Article Analysis Worksheet
After reading the assigned article, please complete this worksheet to prepare for our in-class discussion. Bring a printed copy to class. Please be ready to share your answers with the class.

1. Briefly summarize the article. What interest or question does the author have, what sort of data or evidence does s/he acquire, and what major conclusions (if any) does s/he reach?
2. Was the article written to persuade, propose a solution, give general information, etc.? What was the purpose of the article?
3. Who is the audience?
4. Who is the author/s? Is the author an expert?
5. What newspaper or journal is the article from? Does it contain any bias that you can identify?
6. What is the date of the article? Is it current? Is currency important to this topic?

Discussion Questions (Distributed as a second worksheet, or displayed on the screen)

- List some of the main ideas or key concepts. Think of synonyms and brainstorm related terms that are broader or narrower in scope.
- What researchers, organizations, universities, etc. are concerned with the problem? Are any research studies mentioned?
- What questions came to your mind after reading the article?
- Which disciplines may be interested in studying/exploring this or related topics?

CHAPTER 1
Mapping Scholarly Conversation

KATHLEEN ANNE LANGAN

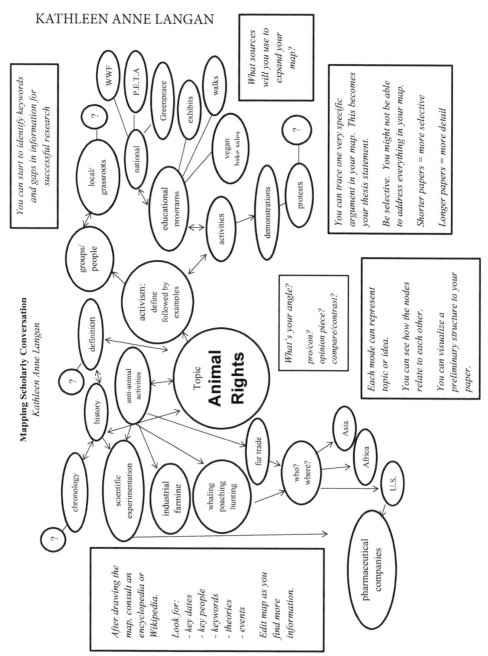

CHAPTER 1
Crafting a Credible Message

DEBBIE MORROW

ROLE 1—HIGH SCHOOL STUDENT

You have an assignment to describe the relationship between smell and memory. Include and explain at least two scientific or technical terms or concepts.

ROLE 2—JOURNALIST

You are researching a feature article for a news magazine or news web site about "DigiScent," a technology to develop "smell-enabled virtual reality."

ROLE 3—PROFESSOR, RESEARCHER, OR SCHOLAR

You are a Psychology PhD with a special research expertise in memory and cognition. You are writing up the results of your most recent experimental study for publication.

ROLE 4—COLLEGE STUDENT

You have an assignment to write a personal reflection on a memory you have that you strongly associate with a particular smell or scent. Frame your reflection with some supporting background information from technical, literary or artistic sources.

Based on the role that you have been assigned from the above list, and using the topic "smells that trigger memories," work with your group or partner to brainstorm a list of sources of information a person in that role would use to find information on that topic. Be sure to consider:

- who you are
- what your message is
- who your audience is

CHAPTER 1
Starting Points: The Role of Blogs in Scholarly Conversation

BRANDON WEST

PART ONE

Author: Name, Position/Occupation, and Affiliated University/Organization

Purpose: Why did the author write this blog entry?

Point of view: How is the author biased? Does the author offer a balanced perspective?

Currency: Are the topics recent? Could the information be outdated?

References: Links or citations referring to other research, studies, or information

Comments: Responses, rebuttals, critiques, questions, or additional information from the blogging community

Names or Organizations: Individual researchers, experts, or other people mentioned

Facts or Data: Information facts for figures, linked or not linked

Blog Roll: What blogs does the blogger follow?

Related Research Ideas: Other topics mentioned in the blog/blog post

Keywords: Relevant ideas/phrases to use to search for more information

PART TWO

AUTHORITY

- What are a few features of this blog that contribute to your understanding of how reliable this blog post or blogger are?
- How would you check on the authority of the blogger?
- How would a casual reader of the blog read the reliability of the blog versus a scholarly reader?
- Who are the scholars who seem to be associated with blog's topic?

SEARCHING

- What are some key words from the blog post you can use to search for more information?
- Using the attributes of this post that you've identified, what are some strategies for finding other information?
- What are some scholarly ways of discovery that you could use to follow up on this or related topics?
- What other topics or questions would you like to answer?

CONVERSATION

- What is evidence of other participants in the conversation?
- What are some of the threads of conversation you see in the blog post you looked at? Does the conversation raise any new ideas or questions?
- Regarding this topic, is there a prevalent point of view?
- Which scholars/practitioners are interested in this topic? Which fields or disciplines are related?

CHAPTER 2
Flawed Questions: Tools for Inquiry

DR. SMITA AVASTHI

Examples of research questions:

- What impact has education had on society?
- My essay will discuss how racism affects a person financially, socially, emotionally, and psychologically.
- Is exercise necessary to maintain a healthy body?
- How has the Internet changed our lives?

Some questions that can be asked to help determine if a research question is appropriate for academic research:

- Can the question be answered yes or no?
- Can the question be answered in one sentence or a single paragraph?
- Have entire books been written to answer this question?
- Would this question be answered by compiling a set of facts or a list?
- Does the question ask for a conclusion to be drawn once the facts are known?
- Would answering this question help someone else who has an interest in this topic?

CHAPTER 2
Developing a Research Question: Topic Selection

KEVIN MICHAEL KLIPFEL

This exercise will help you develop a list of *keywords* you can use to research your topic in article databases and the library catalog:

Summarize the topic you would like to write about in 1–2 sentences:

Identify the key idea in the sentence you wrote above. You may have 1, 2, or 3, depending on your topic.

For each idea, come up with related words or phrases. Think of words and phrases that represent the same idea as the original one.

1: _____Main idea	2: _____Main idea	3: _____Main idea
Keywords or search words	Keywords or search words	Keywords or search words

CHAPTER 3
Evaluating Information Sources

ROBERT FARRELL

- What are you an expert at?

- What did you have to do to acquire that expertise?

- If you meet someone who claims to be expert in the same thing you are, how do you know s/he really is? How do you evaluate her or him?

- What is the difference between what you do to evaluate something in your area of expertise and what you do when you're not an expert?

CHAPTER 3
Determining the Relevance and Reliability of Information Sources

NANCY FAWLEY

Read your assigned source and check all that apply.

Reliable:

_____ Is the author qualified to write about the topic? (Look at her or his credentials, experience, or organizational affiliations.)

_____ Does the URL reveal anything about the author or source?

_____ Is the author trying to sell something?

_____ Does the source reveal a bias?

_____Is the information factual?

_____Are there spelling, grammar or other typographical errors?

_____Is the information current?

Relevant:

_____ Does the information relate to your topic or answer your question?

_____ Does the source meet the requirements of your assignment?

_____ Is the information at an appropriate level (not too elementary or advanced for your needs)?

CHAPTER 3
Non-Scholarly Formats as Research Tools

RACHEL M. MINKIN

- What kind (genre) of writing is this?

- Who's interested in this text? Which majors? Which professionals?

- If we wanted to find out more on this topic, what words (or related terms and words) should we use to search for additional information?

- Thinking about your own possible major, what questions do you have for this author or of the writing?

CHAPTER 3
Scholarly/Non-Scholarly

JO ANGELA OEHRLI & EMILY HAMSTRA

After reading your article, discuss with a partner your answers to the following questions:

1. Who wrote the article?

2. Who reads articles like these?

3. Describe the characteristics of these articles.

4. For what purpose might this article be used?

CHAPTER 4
Using Sources to Support a Claim

DANI BRECHER

THE ARTICLE

- What is the article about? (Summarize in one sentence.)
- For what purpose was it written?
- How long did it take the author to research and write the article?
- Was the article edited?
- Who published it?
- How accurate do you think the factual information in the article is?

CLAIM #1

"*Hail to the Thief* was inspired by not only the political environment of its time, but also by Thom Yorke's interest in earlier 20th century political poets."

- Could you use this article to support this claim? Why or why not?
- If yes, how?
- Is there any bias, tone, etc. that you might need to mention when referencing this source? How might you do so?

CLAIM #2

"Public response to Radiohead's *Hail to the Thief* was colored by the public's strong opinion and memory of the band's previous albums."

- Could you use this article to support this claim? Why or why not?
- If yes, how?
- Is there any bias, tone, etc. that you might need to mention when referencing this source? How might you do so?

CHAPTER 4
Information Life Cycle

TONI M. CARTER & TODD ALDRIDGE

WORKSHEET QUESTIONS

Answer the following questions regarding your source, using the Internet to help you answer if necessary.

1. Who is the author of your source and what are the author's credentials?

2. Who is the intended audience for your source?

3. What is the format of your source? For example, is it a newspaper article, a magazine article, a journal article, etc.

4. How quickly do you think your source can be published? One day, one week, one month, etc?

CHAPTER 5
What is a Database?

SAMANTHA GODBEY, SUE WAINSCOTT, & XAN GOODMAN

Assessment: In last 5 minutes of class, distribute Exit Survey:

1. Are there any questions you still have about databases?

2. Given our lesson today what words come to mind when you think of a database?

3. Before our lesson, how would you rate your comfort with using an academic database?

Not at all   Very comfortable

1	2	3	4	5

4. Now, how would you rate your comfort with using an academic database?

Not at all   Very comfortable

1	2	3	4	5

CHAPTER 5
Who Cares? Understanding the Human Production of Information

REBECCA KUGLITSCH

Briefly state your research topic:

Who would be interested in researching or studying the topic; e.g. specific groups of people and/or organizations?

From what disciplinary lenses might people approach this concept; e.g., public health policy, engineering, materials science?

What kinds of information might the U.S. government collect and provide on this topic?

What other types of information do you think are available on this topic?

How is this information disseminated?

Where would you find it?

CHAPTER 5
Approaching Problems like a Professional

MELISSA MALLON

You are a marketing manager for Whole Foods Market. You've just received word that tomatoes from one of your suppliers might be infected by salmonella. You are asked to provide the company with a report that details how this might affect the company both socially and financially. You remember that this has happened before—a few years ago, the spinach supply was also infected by salmonella. You decide to investigate what happened to the company during this time and if there were any repercussions regarding consumer relations. Work in small groups to answer the following questions.

1. What do you need to know?

2. Where can you locate the information you need?

CHAPTER 5
Databases vs. Search Engines Game

ELIZABETH MARTIN & REBECCA DALY

Name_____   Team_____

Date_____

Research topic/Thesis statement examples:
- Does birth order affect personality?
- In what ways is it important is it for college students to have academic integrity?
- How will climate change affect agricultural systems?
- Should juveniles be sentenced to life in prison?

List keyword or terms that could help focus your research topic.

1. _____

2. _____

3. _____

Find one full-text journal article about the topic. The journal article must have all of the following elements:

Professional Journal (doesn't have to be peer-reviewed)

Name of Journal: _____

Author(s): _____

Date (after 2000):_____

References/Bibliography: Yes_____ No_____

(If No, find an article that does have References.)
Would this article be appropriate for a research paper? Explain why.

CHAPTER 5
Keywording

CATE CALHOUN ORAVET

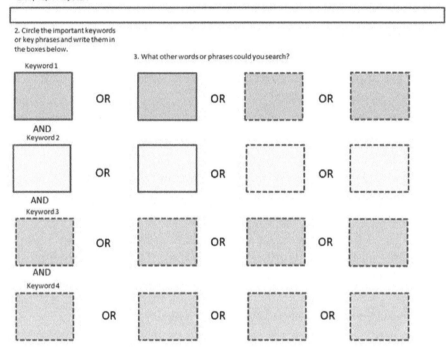

1. My Topic Proposal:

2. Circle the important keywords or key phrases and write them in the boxes below.

3. What other words or phrases could you search?

Keyword 1

OR   OR   OR

AND
Keyword 2

OR   OR   OR

AND
Keyword 3

OR   OR   OR

AND
Keyword 4

OR   OR   OR

CHAPTER 5
Framing a Topic for Library Research

MELISSA BROWNE, CAITLIN PLOVNICK, CATHY PALMER,
RICHARD CALDWELL

1. What is your research question?

2. List as many additional terms/concepts to describe your question as you can:

3. Which subject discipline(s) are likely to have an interest in this question?

4. Are there terms you identified that you think might fit especially well with the subject disciplines you listed?

CHAPTER 5
Framing a Topic for Library Research

MELISSA BROWNE, CAITLIN PLOVNICK, CATHY PALMER,
RICHARD CALDWELL

1. What different types of sources did you find?

2. What audience/discipline is each source intended for?

3. What different terms does each source use for your topic? Are there any that were not in your original list?

CHAPTER 5
Systems of Organization

PETE RAMSEY & STEPHEN "MIKE" KIEL

CHAPTER 6
Gray Areas in Plagiarism Cases

DR. SMITA AVASTHI

SCENARIO 1:

A student borrows a paper from a friend and copies word-for-word several paragraphs where source material is summarized and documented. When confronted by the friend, the student says that the sections she borrowed were just about cited sources so she cannot see the problem. If you were the friend in this case, what would you do?

SCENARIO 2:

A student has written a paper, and the body of it paraphrases another source. There is very little of the student's own writing in the paper, so if s/he documents the source, nearly every paragraph will be cited. A friend points this out when asked to proofread the paper. The paper is due the next morning. What should the student do?

SCENARIO 3:

A student buys a paper off the Internet and is not "caught" by the teacher. This student goes on to work at a respectable newspaper. Years later, his stolen paper is discovered and publicized, and his reputation suffers from this disclosure. What should the editor of the newspaper do?

CHAPTER 6
The Who, What, and Why of the Creative Commons

REBECCA BLIQUEZ & JANE VAN GALEN

SOURCES OF OPEN ACCESS IMAGES

Images from sources on this page are available for use on the open web. You are free to use these images in multimedia projects, websites, blogs, portfolios, etc., that are open and available to the public. When you use these images, you do not need to restrict access to your class or academic environment.

Always read and comply with the use restrictions for specific image sources. Always cite images someone else created. Unless specifically permitted, images should not be sold or used in commercial products or for commercial purposes.

Flickr Create Commons
Flickr contains millions of photographs shared by Flickr users under Creative Commons licenses, and is a strong source for contemporary travel, nature, people, and design photographs. Several overlays to Flickr offer enhanced search functionality and additional features.

- **Flickr Creative Commons** (http://www.flickr.com/creative-commons/)
  Flickr's Creative Commons portal. Browse by license type or choose "Advanced Search" to limit to Creative Commons content.
- **Behold** (http://www.behold.cc/)
- Visual search of Flickr photographs. Uses computer vision to recognize visual content, rather than relying on text tags. Limit to "free to use" or "free to modify."
- **Compfight** (http://compfight.com/)
- Enhanced search of Flickr content. Limit to Creative Commons.
- **FlickrStorm** (http://www.zoo-m.com/flickr-storm/)

- Search overlay to Flickr. Retrieves images more images by using related tags. Select "Advanced" to limit to Creative Commons content.
- **Wylio** (https://www.wylio.com/)
- Searches only Creative Commons content in Flickr. Additional tools for blogs and web sites, including resizing tool, photo credit builder, and code generator.

Open Access Clip Art
- **Open Clip Art Library** (https://openclipart.org/)
- Public domain contemporary graphics contributed by users.
- **Wikimedia Commons—Crystal Clear Icons** (http://commons.wikimedia.org/wiki/Crystal_Clear)
- Icon collection in the Wikimedia Commons.
- **Wikimedia Commons—Tango Icons** (http://commons.wikimedia.org/wiki/Tango_icon)
- Icon collection in the Wikimedia Commons.

Open Access Photographs & Historical Images
- **Library of Congress Prints & Photographs Online** (http://www.loc.gov/pictures/)
- Images from the Library of Congress, now in the public domain.
- **Wikimedia Commons** (http://commons.wikimedia.org/wiki/Main_Page)
- Historical and contemporary images contributed by participants. Millions of high-resolution images of art, architecture, design, people, historical events, diagrams, maps, and more.
- **World Images** (http://worldimages.sjsu.edu/)
- Primarily historical images organized into 18 categories, including women, science, cities, natural world, and more.
- **Yale University Digital Commons** (http://discover.odai.yale.edu/ydc/)
- Yale's digital collections, including images from the Peabody Museum, Center for British Art, University Art Gallery, Library Map Collection, and Walpole Library Prints and Drawings.

Websites with Free Images

These sites offer at least some images for free general use. These sites also contain advertising and/or offer images for sale.

Read each site's conditions for use carefully. Different images from the same site may have different use restrictions, too. Make sure you know what they are.

- **Free Stock Photos** (http://www.freestockphotos.biz/)
- Over 10,000 images, browsable by category. Lots of clip art and clear photographs.
- **morgueFile** (http://www.morguefile.com/)
- Search image tags or browse by category. MorgueFile license clearly explained. Affiliated with dreamstime stock photo.
- **stock.xchng** (http://www.freeimages.com/)
- Stock photography contributed by members. Owned by Getty Images & affiliated wtih iStockphoto.

Metasearch Sites

These sites search multiple other sites for Creative Commons-licensed images. These sites may have ads or offer fee-based services as well.

- **Google Image Search—Usage Rights** (https://images.google. com/)
  Option to search images by content labeled for reuse under a Creative Commons license. Retrieved from a variety of sites/ locations on the web. After you run your search in Images, select 'Search tools' from the Images menu bar and then the appropriate licensing option under 'Usage rights'.
- **evertstockphoto** (http://www.everystockphoto.com/)
  Includes photos from flickr, Wikimedia Commons, morgueFile, and more, with links to original locations. Advanced search allows you to search only the sites you specify.

Adapted from the Copyright Friendly Resources for Media Projects guide, University of Washington Bothell & Cascadia Community College Campus Library: http://libguides. uwb.edu/copyrightfriendly/.

CHAPTER 6
Plagiarism v. Copyright Infringement

PATRICIA BRAVENDER

Plagiarism is "[t]he action or practice of taking someone else's work, idea, etc., and passing it off as one's own; literary theft."[1] Another definition is, "the act of using another person's words or ideas without giving credit to that person."[2]

Copyright is "The right to control the copying, distributing, performing, displaying, and adapting of works (including paintings, music, books, and movies.) The right belongs to the creator, or persons who buy the rights from the creator. This right is created, regulated, and limited by the federal Copyright Act…. and the U.S. Constitution."[3]

Copyright only applies to original works that are fixed in a tangible medium of expression.[4]

Copyright Infringement is "The unauthorized making, using, selling, or distributing of something protected by a…copyright…."[5] Copyright infringement is enforced by the courts and is a legal issue.

SCENARIO 1

Suppose you wrote a poem and posted it on your blog. Someone you do not know wrote music to accompany your poem, and posted a video of a cat lip-synching your poem set to music on YouTube where it became a huge hit.

SCENARIO 2

Suppose you wrote an apocalyptic vampire novel and are selling digital copies on Smashwords for $3.99. It has become a surprise best seller and you are selling hundreds of copies every week. Someone purchased a digital copy from you and then began selling print copies on the Internet through their own personal website. You are still listed as the author.

SCENARIO 3

Suppose you are an amateur photographer and have a web page where you post your best photos. One day you were in the mall and see a calendar for sale that had one of your bird photos on the cover. You are absolutely positive it is the same photo that you posted.

NOTES

1. *Oxford English Dictionary.* http://www.oed.com, s.v. "plagiarism," Accessed November 3, 2014.
2. *Merriam Webster Dictionary,* http://www.merriam-webster.com, s.v. "plagiarism," Accessed November 3, 2014.
3. Daniel Oran, *Oran's Dictionary of the Law,* 4th ed. Clifton Park, N.Y.: Thomson Delmar Learning, 2008, 123, s.v. "copyright."
4. 17 USC §102 (2011).
5. Oran, 267, s.v. "copyright infringement."

CHAPTER 6
Recognizing Plagiarism

PATRICIA BRAVENDER & GAYLE SCHAUB

From Lepore's 4/22/2012 New Yorker article:[1]	From Zakaria's 8/20/2012 Time Magazine column:[2]
As Adam Winkler, a constitutional-law scholar at U.C.L.A., demonstrates in a remarkably nuanced new book, "Gunfight: The Battle Over the Right to Bear Arms in America," firearms have been regulated in the United States from the start. Laws banning the carrying of concealed weapons were passed in Kentucky and Louisiana in 1813, and other states soon followed: Indiana (1820), Tennessee and Virginia (1838), Alabama (1839), and Ohio (1859). Similar laws were passed in Texas, Florida, and Oklahoma. As the governor of Texas explained in 1893, the "mission of the concealed deadly weapon is murder. To check it is the duty of every self-respecting, law-abiding man.	Adam Winkler, a professor of constitutional law at UCLA, documents the actual history in Gunfight: The Battle over the Right to Bear Arms in America. Guns were regulated in the U.S. from the earliest years of the Republic. Laws that banned the carrying of concealed weapons were passed in Kentucky and Louisiana in 1813. Other states soon followed: Indiana in 1820, Tennessee and Virginia in 1838, Alabama in 1839 and Ohio in 1859. Similar laws were passed in Texas, Florida and Oklahoma. As the governor of Texas (Texas!) explained in 1893, the "mission of the concealed deadly weapon is murder. To check it is the duty of every self-respecting, law-abiding man."

Questions to consider:

- What is the problem? Why the accusation of plagiarism?
- How could Zakaria have avoided the accusation?
- Was the penalty fair? What was the effect on his reputation?

NOTES

1. LePore, Jill. "One Nation, Under the Gun." *The New Yorker,* April 23, 2012. http://www.newyorker.com/reporting/2012/04/23/120423fa_fact_lepore?currentPage=all.
2. Zakaria, Fareed. "The Case for Gun Control: Why Limiting Easy Access to Guns is Intelligent and American." *Time,* August 20, 2012, 17.

CHAPTER 6
Louder than Words: Using Infographics to Teach the Value of Information and Authority

HAZEL MCCLURE & CHRISTOPHER TOTH

From the infographic and website where it appears, try to answer the following questions:

- What sources are cited?

- Who is the author?

- What is the purpose of the infographic?

- Who is the intended audience?

- What financial interests are in play?

Using the Internet, try to find:
- Where did this infographic originally appear?

And choose one of the following:
- Check out one of the sources cited. Does it appear legitimate? How can you tell?

- Choose one fact that is included in the infographic. Try to find a different source that confirms this fact.

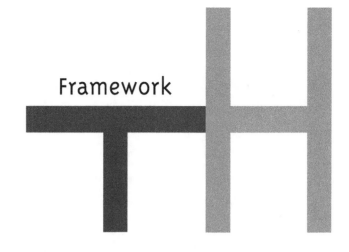

Framework

Framework for Information Literacy for Higher Education

Filed by the ACRL Board of Directors as one of the constellation of information literacy documents from the association on February 2, 2015.

CONTENTS

These six frames are presented alphabetically and do not suggest a particular sequence in which they must be learned.

Introduction

This *Framework for Information Literacy for Higher Education* (*Framework*) grows out of a belief that information literacy as an educational reform movement will realize its potential only through a richer, more complex set of core ideas. During the fifteen years since the publication of the *Information Literacy Competency Standards for Higher Education*,[1] academic librarians and their partners in higher education associations have developed learning outcomes, tools, and resources that some institutions have deployed to infuse information literacy concepts and skills into their curricula. However, the rapidly changing higher education environment, along with the dynamic and often uncertain information ecosystem in which all of us work and live, require new attention to be focused on foundational ideas about that ecosystem. Students have a greater role and responsibility in creating new knowledge, in understanding the contours and the changing dynamics of the world of information, and in using information, data, and scholarship ethically. Teaching faculty have a greater responsibility in designing curricula and assignments that foster enhanced engagement with the core ideas about information and scholarship within their disciplines. Librarians have a greater responsibility in identifying core ideas within their own knowledge domain that can extend learning for students, in creating a new cohesive curriculum for information literacy, and in collaborating more extensively with faculty.

The *Framework* offered here is called a framework intentionally because it is based on a cluster of interconnected core concepts, with flexible options for implementation, rather than on a set of standards, learning outcomes, or any prescriptive enumeration of skills. At the heart of this *Framework* are conceptual understandings that organize many other concepts and ideas about information, research, and scholarship into a coherent whole. These conceptual understandings are informed by the work of Wiggins and McTighe,[2] which focuses on essential concepts and questions in developing curricula and focuses on *threshold concepts*.[3] Threshold concepts are those ideas in any discipline that are passageways or portals to enlarged understanding or ways of thinking and practicing within that discipline. This *Framework* draws upon an ongoing Delphi Study that has identified several threshold concepts in information literacy,[4] but the *Framework* has been molded using fresh ideas and emphases for the threshold concepts. Two added elements illustrate important learning goals related to those concepts: *knowledge practices*,[5] which are demonstrations of ways in which learners can increase their understanding of these information literacy concepts and *dispositions*,[6] which describe ways in which to address the affective, attitudinal, or valuing dimension of learning. The *Framework* is organized into six frames, each consisting of a concept central to information literacy, a set of knowledge practices, and a set of dispositions. The six concepts that anchor the frames are presented alphabetically:

1. Authority Is Constructed and Contextual
2. Information Creation as a Process
3. Information Has Value
4. Research as Inquiry
5. Scholarship as Conversation
6. Searching as Strategic Exploration

Neither the knowledge practices nor the dispositions that support each concept are intended to prescribe what local institutions should do in using the *Framework*; each library and its partners on campus will need to deploy these frames to best fit their own situation, including designing learning outcomes. For the same reason, these lists should not be considered exhaustive.

In addition, this *Framework* draws significantly upon the concept of metaliteracy,[7] which offers a renewed vision of information literacy as an overarching set of abilities in which students are consumers and creators of information who can participate successfully in collaborative spaces.[8] Metaliteracy demands behavioral, affective, cognitive, and metacognitive engagement with the information ecosystem. This *Framework* depends on these core ideas of metaliteracy, with special focus on metacognition,[9] or critical self-reflection, as crucial to becoming more self-directed in that rapidly changing ecosystem.

Because this *Framework* envisions information literacy as extending the arc of learning throughout students' academic careers and as converging with other academic and social learning goals, an expanded definition of information literacy is offered here to emphasize dynamism, flexibility, individual growth, and community learning:

> Information literacy is the set of integrated abilities encompassing the reflective discovery of information, the understanding of how information is produced and valued, and the use of information in creating new knowledge and participating ethically in communities of learning.

The *Framework* opens the way for librarians, faculty, and other institutional partners to redesign instruction sessions, assignments, courses, and even curricula; to connect information literacy with student success initiatives; to collaborate on pedagogical research and involve students themselves in that research; and to create wider conversations about student learning, the scholarship of teaching and learning, and the assessment of learning on local campuses and beyond.

NOTES

1. Association of College & Research Libraries, Information Literacy Competency Standards for Higher Education (Chicago, 2000).
2. Grant Wiggins and Jay McTighe. *Understanding by Design*. (Alexandria, VA: Association for Supervision and Curriculum Development, 2004).
3. Threshold concepts are core or foundational concepts that, once grasped by the learner, create new perspectives and ways of understanding a discipline or challenging knowledge domain. Such concepts produce transformation within the learner; without them, the learner does not acquire expertise in that field of knowledge. Threshold concepts can be thought of as portals through which the learner must pass to develop new perspectives and wider understanding. Jan H. F. Meyer, Ray Land,

and Caroline Baillie. "Editors' Preface." In *Threshold Concepts and Transformational Learning*, edited by Jan H. F. Meyer, Ray Land, and Caroline Baillie, ix–xlii. (Rotterdam, Netherlands: Sense Publishers, 2010).

4. For information on this unpublished, in-progress Delphi Study on threshold concepts and information literacy, conducted by Lori Townsend, Amy Hofer, Silvia Lu, and Korey Brunetti, see http://www.ilthresholdconcepts.com/. Lori Townsend, Korey Brunetti, and Amy R. Hofer. "Threshold Concepts and Information Literacy." *portal: Libraries and the Academy* 11, no. 3 (2011): 853–69.

5. Knowledge practices are the proficiencies or abilities that learners develop as a result of their comprehending a threshold concept.

6. Generally, a disposition is a tendency to act or think in a particular way. More specifically, a disposition is a cluster of preferences, attitudes, and intentions, as well as a set of capabilities that allow the preferences to become realized in a particular way. Gavriel Salomon. "To Be or Not to Be (Mindful)." Paper presented at the American Educational Research Association Meetings, New Orleans, LA, 1994.

7. Metaliteracy expands the scope of traditional information skills (i.e., determine, access, locate, understand, produce, and use information) to include the collaborative production and sharing of information in participatory digital environments (collaborate, produce, and share). This approach requires an ongoing adaptation to emerging technologies and an understanding of the critical thinking and reflection required to engage in these spaces as producers, collaborators, and distributors. Thomas P. Mackey and Trudi E. Jacobson. *Metaliteracy: Reinventing Information Literacy to Empower Learners.* (Chicago: Neal-Schuman, 2014).

8. Thomas P. Mackey and Trudi E. Jacobson. "Reframing Information Literacy as a Metaliteracy." *College and Research Libraries* 72, no. 1 (2011): 62–78.

9. Metacognition is an awareness and understanding of one's own thought processes. It focuses on how people learn and process information, taking into consideration people's awareness of how they learn. (Jennifer A. Livingston. "Metacognition: An Overview." Online paper, State University of New York at Buffalo, Graduate School of Education, 1997. http://gse.buffalo.edu/fas/shuell/cep564/metacog.htm.)

Authority Is Constructed and Contextual

Information resources reflect their creators' expertise and credibility, and are evaluated based on the information need and the context in which the information will be used. Authority is constructed in that various communities may recognize different types of authority. It is contextual in that the information need may help to determine the level of authority required.

Experts understand that authority is a type of influence recognized or exerted within a community. Experts view authority with an attitude of informed skepticism and an openness to new perspectives, additional voices, and changes in schools of thought. Experts understand the need to determine the validity of the information created by different authorities and to acknowledge biases that privilege some sources of authority over others, especially in terms of others' worldviews, gender, sexual orientation, and cultural orientations. An understanding of this concept enables novice learners to critically examine all evidence—be it a short blog post or a peer-reviewed conference proceeding—and to ask relevant questions about origins, context, and suitability for the current information need. Thus, novice learners come to respect the expertise that authority represents while remaining skeptical of the systems that have elevated that authority and the information created by it. Experts know how to seek authoritative voices but also recognize that unlikely voices can be authoritative, depending on need. Novice learners may need to rely on basic indicators of authority, such as type of publication or author credentials, where experts recognize schools of thought or discipline-specific paradigms.

KNOWLEDGE PRACTICES

Learners who are developing their information literate abilities do the following:

- Define different types of authority, such as subject expertise (e.g., scholarship), societal position (e.g., public office or title), or special experience (e.g., participating in a historic event).
- Use research tools and indicators of authority to determine the credibility of sources, understanding the elements that might temper this credibility.

- Understand that many disciplines have acknowledged authorities in the sense of well-known scholars and publications that are widely considered "standard". Even in those situations, some scholars would challenge the authority of those sources.
- Recognize that authoritative content may be packaged formally or informally and may include sources of all media types.
- Acknowledge they are developing their own authoritative voices in a particular area and recognize the responsibilities this entails, including seeking accuracy and reliability, respecting intellectual property, and participating in communities of practice.
- Understand the increasingly social nature of the information ecosystem where authorities actively connect with one another and sources develop over time.

DISPOSITIONS

Learners who are developing their information literate abilities do the following:

- Develop and maintain an open mind when encountering varied and sometimes conflicting perspectives
- Motivate themselves to find authoritative sources, recognizing that authority may be conferred or manifested in unexpected ways
- Develop awareness of the importance of assessing content with a skeptical stance and with a self-awareness of their own biases and worldview
- Question traditional notions of granting authority and recognize the value of diverse ideas and worldviews
- Are conscious that maintaining these attitudes and actions requires frequent self-evaluation

Information Creation as a Process

Information in any format is produced to convey a message and is shared via a selected delivery method. The iterative processes of researching, creating, revising, and disseminating information vary, and the resulting product reflects these differences.

The information creation process could result in a range of information formats and modes of delivery, so experts look beyond format when selecting resources to use. The unique capabilities and constraints of each creation process as well as the specific information need determine how the product is used. Experts recognize that information creations are valued differently in different contexts, such as academia or the workplace. Elements that affect or reflect on the creation, such as a pre- or post-publication editing or reviewing process, may be indicators of quality. The dynamic nature of information creation and dissemination requires ongoing attention to understand evolving creation processes. Recognizing the nature of information creation, experts look to the underlying processes of creation as well as the final product to critically evaluate the usefulness of the information. Novice learners begin to recognize the significance of the creation process, leading them to increasingly sophisticated choices when matching information products with their information needs.

KNOWLEDGE PRACTICES

Learners who are developing their information literate abilities do the following:

- Articulate the capabilities and constraints of information developed through various creation processes
- Assess the fit between an information product's creation process and a particular information need
- Articulate the traditional and emerging processes of information creation and dissemination in a particular discipline
- Recognize that information may be perceived differently based on the format in which it is packaged
- Recognize the implications of information formats that contain static or dynamic information

- Monitor the value that is placed upon different types of information products in varying contexts
- Transfer knowledge of capabilities and constraints to new types of information products
- Develop, in their own creation processes, an understanding that their choices impact the purposes for which the information product will be used and the message it conveys

DISPOSITIONS

Learners who are developing their information literate abilities do the following:

- Are inclined to seek out characteristics of information products that indicate the underlying creation process
- Value the process of matching an information need with an appropriate product
- Accept that the creation of information may begin initially through communicating in a range of formats or modes
- Accept the ambiguity surrounding the potential value of information creation expressed in emerging formats or modes
- Resist the tendency to equate format with the underlying creation process
- Understand that different methods of information dissemination with different purposes are available for their use

Information Has Value

Information possesses several dimensions of value, including as a commodity, as a means of education, as a means to influence, and as a means of negotiating and understanding the world. Legal and socioeconomic interests influence information production and dissemination.

The value of information is manifested in various contexts, including publishing practices, information access, the commodification of personal information, and intellectual property laws. The novice learner may struggle to understand the diverse values of information in an environment where "free" information and related services are plentiful and the concept of intellectual property is first encountered through rules of citation or warnings about plagiarism and copyright law. As creators and users of information, experts understand their rights and responsibilities when participating in a community of scholarship. Experts understand that value may be wielded by powerful interests in ways that marginalize certain voices. However, value may be leveraged by individuals and organizations to effect change and may be leveraged for civic, economic, social, or personal gains. Experts also understand the individual is responsible for making deliberate and informed choices about when to comply with and when to contest current legal and socioeconomic practices concerning the value of information.

KNOWLEDGE PRACTICES

Learners who are developing their information literate abilities do the following:

- Give credit to the original ideas of others through proper attribution and citation
- Understand that intellectual property is a legal and social construct that varies by culture
- Articulate the purpose and distinguishing characteristics of copyright, fair use, open access, and the public domain
- Understand how and why some individuals or groups of individuals may be underrepresented or systematically marginalized within the systems that produce and disseminate information

- Recognize issues of access or lack of access to information sources
- Decide where and how their information is published
- Understand how the commodification of their personal information and online interactions affects the information they receive and the information they produce or disseminate online
- Make informed choices regarding their online actions in full awareness of issues related to privacy and the commodification of personal information

DISPOSITIONS

Learners who are developing their information literate abilities do the following:

- Respect the original ideas of others
- Value the skills, time, and effort needed to produce knowledge
- See themselves as contributors to the information marketplace rather than only consumers of it
- Are inclined to examine their own information privilege

Research as Inquiry

Research is iterative and depends upon asking increasingly complex or new questions whose answers in turn develop additional questions or lines of inquiry in any field.

Experts see inquiry as a process that focuses on problems or questions in a discipline or between open or unresolved disciplines. Experts recognize the collaborative effort within a discipline to extend the knowledge in that field. Many times, this process includes points of disagreement where debate and dialogue work to deepen the conversations around knowledge. This process of inquiry extends beyond the academic world to the community at large, and the process of inquiry may focus upon personal, professional, or societal needs. The spectrum of inquiry ranges from asking simple questions that depend upon basic recapitulation of knowledge to increasingly sophisticated abilities to refine research questions, use more advanced research methods, and explore more diverse disciplinary perspectives. Novice learners acquire strategic perspectives on inquiry and a greater repertoire of investigative methods.

KNOWLEDGE PRACTICES

Learners who are developing their information literate abilities do the following:

- Formulate questions for research based on information gaps or on reexamination of existing, possibly conflicting, information
- Determine an appropriate scope of investigation
- Deal with complex research by breaking complex questions into simple ones, limiting the scope of investigations
- Use various research methods, based on need, circumstance, and type of inquiry
- Monitor gathered information and assess for gaps or weaknesses
- Organize information in meaningful ways
- Synthesize ideas gathered from multiple sources
- Draw reasonable conclusions based on the analysis and interpretation of information

DISPOSITIONS

Learners who are developing their information literate abilities do the following:

- Consider research as open-ended exploration and engagement with information
- Appreciate that a question may appear to be simple but still disruptive and important to research
- Value intellectual curiosity in developing questions and learning new investigative methods
- Maintain an open mind and a critical stance
- Value persistence, adaptability, and flexibility and recognize that ambiguity can benefit the research process
- Seek multiple perspectives during information gathering and assessment
- Seek appropriate help when needed
- Follow ethical and legal guidelines in gathering and using information
- Demonstrate intellectual humility (i.e., recognize their own intellectual or experiential limitations)

Scholarship as Conversation

Communities of scholars, researchers, or professionals engage in sustained discourse with new insights and discoveries occurring over time as a result of varied perspectives and interpretations.

Research in scholarly and professional fields is a discursive practice in which ideas are formulated, debated, and weighed against one another over an extended time. Instead of seeking discrete answers to complex problems, experts understand that a given issue may be characterized by several competing perspectives as part of an ongoing conversation in which information users and creators come together and negotiate meaning. Experts understand that, though some topics have established answers through this process, a query may have more than one uncontested answer. Experts are, therefore, inclined to seek out many perspectives, not merely the ones with which they are familiar. These perspectives might be in their own discipline or profession or may be in other fields. Even though novice learners and experts at all levels can take part in the conversation, established power and authority structures may influence their ability to participate and can privilege certain voices and information. Developing familiarity with the sources of evidence, methods, and modes of discourse in the field assists novice learners to enter the conversation. New forms of scholarly and research conversations provide more avenues in which a wide variety of individuals may have a voice in the conversation. Providing attribution to relevant previous research is also an obligation of participation in the conversation. It enables the conversation to move forward and strengthens one's voice in the conversation.

KNOWLEDGE PRACTICES

Learners who are developing their information literate abilities do the following:

- Cite the contributing work of others in their own information production
- Contribute to scholarly conversation at an appropriate level, such as local online community, guided discussion, undergraduate research journal, conference presentation/poster session

- Identify barriers to entering scholarly conversation via various venues
- Critically evaluate contributions made by others in participatory information environments
- Identify the contribution particular articles, books, and other scholarly pieces make to disciplinary knowledge
- Summarize the changes in scholarly perspective over time on a particular topic within a specific discipline
- Recognize that a given scholarly work may not represent the only or even the majority perspective on the issue

DISPOSITIONS

Learners who are developing their information literate abilities do the following:

- Recognize they are often entering into an ongoing scholarly conversation and not a finished conversation
- Seek out conversations taking place in their research area
- See themselves as contributors to scholarship rather than only consumers of it
- Recognize that scholarly conversations take place in various venues
- Suspend judgment on the value of a particular piece of scholarship until the larger context for the scholarly conversation is better understood
- Understand the responsibility that comes with entering the conversation through participatory channels
- Value user-generated content and evaluate contributions made by others
- Recognize that systems **privilege** authorities and that not having a fluency in the language and process of a discipline disempowers their ability to participate and engage

Searching as Strategic Exploration

Searching for information is often nonlinear and iterative, requiring the evaluation of a range of information sources and the mental flexibility to pursue alternate avenues as new understanding develops.

The act of searching often begins with a question that directs the act of finding needed information. Encompassing inquiry, discovery, and serendipity, searching identifies possible relevant sources and the means to access those sources. Experts realize that information searching is a contextualized, complex experience that affects, and is affected by, the searcher's cognitive, affective, and social dimensions. Novice learners may search a limited set of resources, and experts may search more broadly and deeply to determine the most appropriate information within the project scope. Likewise, novice learners tend to use few search strategies; experts select from various search strategies, depending on the sources, scope, and context of the information need.

KNOWLEDGE PRACTICES

Learners who are developing their information literate abilities do the following:

- Determine the initial scope of the task required to meet their information needs
- Identify interested parties, such as scholars, organizations, governments, and industries, which might produce information about a topic and determine how to access that information
- Utilize divergent (e.g., brainstorming) and convergent (e.g., selecting the best source) thinking when searching
- Match information needs and search strategies to search tools
- Design and refine needs and search strategies, based on search results
- Understand how information systems (i.e., collections of recorded information) are organized to access relevant information
- Use different searching language types (e.g., controlled vocabulary, keywords, natural language)
- Manage searching processes and results

DISPOSITIONS

Learners who are developing their information literate abilities do the following:

- Exhibit mental flexibility and creativity
- Understand that first attempts at searching do not always produce adequate results
- Realize that information sources vary greatly in content and format and have varying relevance and value, depending on the needs and nature of the search
- Seek guidance from experts, such as librarians, researchers, and professionals
- Recognize the value of browsing and other serendipitous methods of information gathering
- Persist in the face of search challenges, and know when enough information completes the information task

APPENDIX F1: IMPLEMENTING THE FRAMEWORK
Suggestions on How to Use the Framework for Information Literacy for Higher Education

The *Framework* is a mechanism for guiding the development of information literacy programs within higher education institutions while promoting discussion about the nature of key concepts in information in general education and disciplinary studies. The *Framework* encourages thinking about how librarians, faculty, and others can address core or portal concepts and associated elements in the information field within the context of higher education. The *Framework* will help librarians contextualize and integrate information literacy for their institutions and will encourage a deeper understanding of what knowledge practices and dispositions an information literate student should develop. The *Framework* redefines the boundaries of what librarians teach and how they conceptualize the study of information within the curricula of higher education institutions.

The *Framework* has been conceived as a set of living documents on which the profession will build. The key product is a set of frames, or lenses, through which to view information literacy, each of which includes a concept central to information literacy, knowledge practices, and dispositions. The Association of College & Research Libraries (ACRL) encourages the library community to discuss the new *Framework* widely and to develop resources such as curriculum guides, concept maps, and assessment instruments to supplement the core set of materials in the frames.

As a first step, the ACRL encourages librarians to read through the entire *Framework* and discuss the implications of this approach for the information literacy program at their institution. Possibilities include convening a discussion among librarians at an institution or joining an online discussion of librarians. In addition, as one becomes familiar with the frames, consider discussing them with professionals in the institution's center for teaching and learning, office of undergraduate education, or similar departments to see whether some synergies exist between this approach and other institutional curricular initiatives.

The frames can guide the redesign of information literacy programs for general education courses, for upper level courses in students' major departments, and for graduate student education. The frames are intended to demonstrate the contrast in thinking between *novice learner* and *expert* in a specific area; movement may take place over the course of a student's academic career. Mapping out in what way specific concepts will be integrated into specific curriculum levels is one of the challenges of implementing the *Framework*. The ACRL encourages librarians to work with faculty, departmental or college curriculum committees, instructional designers, staff from centers for teaching and learning, and others to design information literacy programs in a holistic way.

The ACRL realizes that many information literacy librarians currently meet with students via one-shot classes, especially in introductory level classes. Over the course of a student's academic program, one-shot sessions that address a particular need at a particular time, systematically integrated into the curriculum, can play a significant role in an information literacy program. Librarians and teaching faculty must understand that the *Framework* is not designed to be implemented in a single information literacy session in a student's academic career; it is intended to be developmentally and systematically integrated into the student's academic program at various levels. This may take considerable time to implement fully in many institutions.

The ACRL encourages information literacy librarians to be imaginative and innovative in implementing the *Framework* in their institution. The *Framework* is not intended to be prescriptive but to be used as a guidance document in shaping an institutional program. The ACRL recommends piloting the implementation of the *Framework* in a context useful to a specific institution, assessing the results and sharing experiences with colleagues.

HOW TO USE THIS FRAMEWORK

- Read and reflect on the entire *Framework* document.

- Convene or join a group of librarians to discuss the implications of this approach to information literacy for your institution.
- Reach out to potential partners in your institution, such as departmental curriculum committees, centers for teaching and learning, or offices of undergraduate or graduate studies, to discuss how to implement the *Framework* in your institutional context.
- Using the *Framework*, pilot the development of information literacy sessions within a particular academic program in your institution. Assess and share the results with your colleagues.
- Share instructional materials with other information literacy librarians in the online repository developed by the ACRL.

Introduction for Faculty and Administrators

CONSIDERING INFORMATION LITERACY

Information literacy is the set of integrated abilities encompassing the reflective discovery of information, the understanding of how information is produced and valued, and the use of information in creating new knowledge and participating ethically in communities of learning.

This *Framework* sets forth these information literacy concepts and describes how librarians as information professionals can facilitate the development of information literacy by postsecondary students.

CREATING A FRAMEWORK

The ACRL has played a leading role in promoting information literacy in higher education for decades. The *Information Literacy Competency Standards for Higher Education* (*Standards*), first published in 2000, enabled colleges and universities to position information literacy as an essential learning outcome in the curriculum and promoted linkages with general education programs, service learning, problem-based learning, and other pedagogies focused on deeper learning. Regional accrediting bodies, the

American Association of Colleges and Universities (AAC&U), and various discipline-specific organizations employed and adapted the *Standards*.

It is time for a fresh look at information literacy, especially in light of changes in higher education, coupled with increasingly complex information ecosystems. To that end, an ACRL Task Force developed the *Framework*. The *Framework* seeks to address the great potential for information literacy as a deeper, more integrated learning agenda, addressing academic and technical courses, undergraduate research, community-based learning, and cocurricular learning experiences of entering freshman through graduation. The *Framework* focuses attention on the vital role of collaboration and its potential for increasing student understanding of the processes of knowledge creation and scholarship. The *Framework* also emphasizes student participation and creativity, highlighting the importance of these contributions.

The *Framework* is developed around a set of "frames," which are those gateway or portal concepts through which students must pass to develop genuine expertise within a discipline, profession, or knowledge domain. Each frame includes a knowledge practices section used to demonstrate how the mastery of the concept leads to application in new situations and knowledge generation. Each frame also includes a set of dispositions that address the affective areas of learning.

For Faculty: How to Use the Framework

A vital benefit in using threshold concepts as one of the underpinnings for the *Framework* is the potential for collaboration among disciplinary faculty, librarians, teaching and learning center staff, and others. Creating a community of conversations about this enlarged understanding should engender more collaboration, more innovative course designs, and a more inclusive consideration of learning within and beyond the classroom. Threshold concepts originated as faculty pedagogical research within disciplines. Because information literacy is a disciplinary and a transdisciplinary learning agenda, using a conceptual framework for information literacy program planning, librarian-faculty collaboration, and student cocurricular projects can offer great potential for curricular enrichment and transformation. As a faculty member, you can take the following approaches:

- Investigate threshold concepts in your discipline and gain an understanding of the approach used in the *Framework* as it applies to the discipline you know.

  —What are the specialized information skills in your discipline that students should develop, such as using primary sources (history) or accessing and managing large data sets (science)?

- Look for workshops at your campus teaching and learning center on the flipped classroom and consider how such practices could be incorporated into your courses.

  —What information and research assignments can students do outside of class to arrive prepared to apply concepts and conduct collaborative projects?

- Partner with your IT department and librarians to develop new kinds of multimedia assignments for courses.

  —What kinds of workshops and other services should be available for students involved in multimedia design and production?

- Help students view themselves as information producers, individually and collaboratively.

  —In your program, how do students interact with, evaluate, produce, and share information in various formats and modes?

- Consider the knowledge practices and dispositions in each information literacy frame for possible integration into your own courses and academic program.

  —How might you and a librarian design learning experiences and assignments that will encourage students to assess their own attitudes, strengths/weaknesses, and knowledge gaps related to information?

For Administrators: How to Support the Framework

Through reading the *Framework* document and discussing it with your institutions' librarians, you can focus on the best mechanisms to implement the *Framework* in your institution. As an administrator, you can take the following approaches:

- Host or encourage a series of campus conversations about how the institution can incorporate the *Framework* into student learning outcomes and supporting curriculum
- Provide the resources to enhance faculty expertise and opportunities for understanding and incorporating the *Framework* into the curriculum
- Encourage committees working on planning documents related to teaching and learning (at the department, program, and institutional levels) to include concepts from the *Framework* in their work
- Provide resources to support a meaningful assessment of information literacy of students at various levels at your institution
- Promote partnerships between faculty, librarians, instructional designers, and others to develop meaningful ways for students to become content creators, especially in their disciplines

APPENDIX F2: BACKGROUND OF THE FRAMEWORK DEVELOPMENT

The *Standards* were published in 2000 and brought information literacy into higher education conversations and advanced our field. These, like all ACRL standards, are reviewed cyclically. In July 2011, ACRL appointed a Task Force to decide what to do with the current *Standards*. In June 2012, that Task Force recommended revising the current *Standards*. This previous review Task Force made recommendations that informed the current revision Task Force, created in 2013, with the following charge:

> to update the Standards so they reflect the current thinking on such things as the creation and dissemination of knowledge, the changing global higher education and learning environment, the shift from information literacy to information fluency, and the expanding definition of information literacy to include multiple literacies, for example, transliteracy, media literacy, digital literacy, etc.

Two new elements underlie the model that has been developed: threshold concepts and metaliteracy. The Task Force released the first version of the *Framework* in two parts in February and April of 2014 and received comments via two online hearings and a feedback form available online for four weeks. The committee revised the document, released the second draft on June 17, 2014, and sought extensive feedback through a feedback form, two online hearings, an in-person hearing, and analysis of social media and topical blog posts.

On a regular basis, the Task Force used all of the ACRL's and American Library Association's (ALA) communication channels to reach individual members and ALA and ACRL units (committees, sections, round tables, ethnic caucuses, chapters, and divisions) with updates. The Task Force's liaison at ACRL maintained a private e-mail distribution list of over 1,300 individuals who attended a fall, spring, or summer online forum; provided comments to the February, April, June, or November drafts; or were otherwise identified as having strong interest and expertise. This included members of the Task Force that drafted the *Standards*, leading Library Information Science (LIS) researchers and national project directors, members of the Information Literacy Rubric Development Team for the Association of American Colleges & Universities, and Valid Assessment of Learning in Undergraduate Education initiative. Via all these channels, the Task Force regularly shared updates, invited discussion at virtual and in-person forums and hearings, and encouraged comments on public drafts of the proposed *Framework*.

The ACRL recognized that the effect of any changes to the *Standards* would be significant within the library profession and in higher education more broadly. In addition to general announcements, the Task Force contacted nearly 60 researchers who cited the *Standards* in publications outside LIS literature, more than 70 deans, associate deans, directors or chairs of LIS schools, and invited specific staff leaders (and press or communications contacts) at more than 70 other higher education associations, accrediting agencies, and library associations and consortia to encourage their members to read and comment on the draft.

The Task Force systematically reviewed feedback from the first and second drafts of the *Framework*, including comments, criticism, and praise provided through formal and informal channels. The three official online feedback forms had 562 responses; numerous direct e-mails were sent to members of the Task Force. The group was proactive in tracking feedback on social media, namely blog posts and Twitter. While the data harvested from social media are not exhaustive, the Task Force made its best efforts to include all known Twitter conversations, blog posts, and blog commentary. In total, there were several hundred feedback documents, totaling over a thousand pages, under review. The content of these documents was analyzed by members of the Task Force and coded using HyperResearch, a qualitative data analysis software. During the drafting and vetting process, the Task Force provided more detail on the feedback analysis in an online FAQ document.

The Task Force continued to revise the document and published the third revision in November 2014, again announcing broadly and seeking comments via a feedback form.

As of November 2014, the Task Force members included the following:

- Craig Gibson, Professor, Ohio State University Libraries (Co-chair)
- Trudi E. Jacobson, Distinguished Librarian and Head, Information Literacy Department, University at Albany, SUNY, University Libraries (Co-chair)
- Elizabeth Berman, Science and Engineering Librarian, University of Vermont (Member)
- Carl O. DiNardo, Assistant Professor and Coordinator of Library Instruction/Science Librarian, Eckerd College (Member)
- Lesley S. J. Farmer, Professor, California State University–Long Beach (Member)
- Ellie A. Fogarty, Vice President, Middle States Commission on Higher Education (Member)
- Diane M. Fulkerson, Social Sciences and Education Librarian, University of South Florida in Lakeland (Member)
- Merinda Kaye Hensley, Instructional Services Librarian and Scholarly Commons Co-coordinator, University of Illinois at Urbana-Champaign (Member)
- Joan K. Lippincott, Associate Executive Director, Coalition for Networked Information (Member)
- Michelle S. Millet, Library Director, John Carroll University (Member)
- Troy Swanson, Teaching and Learning Librarian, Moraine Valley Community College (Member)
- Lori Townsend, Data Librarian for Social Sciences and Humanities, University of New Mexico (Member)
- Julie Ann Garrison, Associate Dean of Research and Instructional Services, Grand Valley State University (Board Liaison)
- Kate Ganski, Library Instruction Coordinator, University of Wisconsin–Milwaukee (Visiting Program Officer, from September 1, 2013, through June 30, 2014)
- Kara Malenfant, Senior Strategist for Special Initiatives, Association of College and Research Libraries (Staff Liaison)

In December 2014, the Task Force made final changes. Two other ACRL groups reviewed and provided feedback on the final drafts: the ACRL Information Literacy Standards Committee and the ACRL Standards Committee. The latter group submitted the final document and recommendations to the ACRL Board for its review at the 2015 ALA Midwinter Meeting in Chicago.

APPENDIX F3: SOURCES FOR FURTHER READING

The following sources are suggested readings for those who want to learn more about the ideas underpinning the *Framework*, especially the use of threshold concepts and related pedagogical models. Some readings here explore other models for information literacy, discuss students' challenges with information literacy, or offer examples of assessment of threshold concepts. Landmark works on threshold concept theory and research on this list are the edited volumes by Meyer, Land, and Baillie (*Threshold Concepts and Transformational Learning*) and by Meyer and Land (*Threshold Concepts and Troublesome Knowledge: Linkages to Ways of Thinking and Practicing within the Disciplines*). In addition, numerous research articles, conference papers, reports, and presentations on threshold concepts are cited on the regularly updated website Threshold Concepts: Undergraduate Teaching, Postgraduate Training, and Professional Development; A Short Introduction and Bibliography, available at http://www.ee.ucl.ac.uk/~mflanaga/thresholds.html.

ACRL Information Literacy Competency Standards Review Task Force. "Task Force Recommendations." ACRL AC12 Doc 13.1, June 2, 2012. http://www.ala.org/acrl/sites/ala.org.acrl/files/content/standards/ils_recomm.pdf.

American Association for School Librarians. *Standards for the 21st-Century Learner*. Chicago: American Library Association, 2007. http://www.ala.org/aasl/sites/ala.org.aasl/files/content/guidelinesandstandards/learningstandards/AASL_LearningStandards.pdf.

Blackmore, Margaret. "Student Engagement with Information: Applying a Threshold Concept Approach to Information Literacy Development." Paper presented at the 3rd Biennial Threshold Concepts Symposium: Exploring Transformative Dimensions of Threshold Concepts, Sydney, Australia, July 1–2, 2010.

Carmichael, Patrick. "Tribes, Territories, and Threshold Concepts: Educational Materialisms at Work in Higher Education."

Educational Philosophy and Theory 44, no. S1 (2012): 31–42.

Coonan, Emma. *A New Curriculum for Information Literacy: Teaching Learning; Perceptions of Information Literacy.* Arcadia Project, Cambridge University Library, July 2011. http://ccfil.pbworks.com/f/emma_report_final.pdf.

Cousin, Glynis. "An Introduction to Threshold Concepts." *Planet* 17 (December 2006): 4–5.

———. "Threshold Concepts, Troublesome Knowledge and Emotional Capital: An Exploration into Learning about Others." In *Overcoming Barriers to Student Understanding: Threshold Concepts and Troublesome Knowledge,* edited by Jan H. F. Meyer and Ray Land, 134–47. London and New York: Routledge, 2006.

Gibson, Craig, and Trudi Jacobson. "Informing and Extending the Draft ACRL Information Literacy Framework for Higher Education: An Overview and Avenues for Research." *College and Research Libraries* 75, no. 3 (May 2014): 250–4.

Head, Alison J. "Project Information Literacy: What Can Be Learned about the Information-Seeking Behavior of Today's College Students?" Paper presented at the ACRL National Conference, Indianapolis, IN, April 10–13, 2013.

Hofer, Amy R., Lori Townsend, and Korey Brunetti. "Troublesome Concepts and Information Literacy: Investigating Threshold Concepts for IL Instruction." *portal: Libraries and the Academy* 12, no. 4 (2012): 387–405.

Jacobson, Trudi E., and Thomas P. Mackey. "Proposing a Metaliteracy Model to Redefine Information Literacy." *Communications in Information Literacy* 7, no. 2 (2013): 84–91.

Kuhlthau, Carol C. "Rethinking the 2000 ACRL Standards: Some Things to Consider." *Communications in Information Literacy* 7, no. 3 (2013): 92–7.

———. *Seeking Meaning: A Process Approach to Library and Information Services.* Westport, CT: Libraries Unlimited, 2004.

Limberg, Louise, Mikael Alexandersson, Annika Lantz-Andersson, and Lena Folkesson. "What Matters? Shaping Meaningful Learning through Teaching Information Literacy." *Libri* 58, no. 2 (2008): 82–91.

Lloyd, Annemaree. *Information Literacy Landscapes: Information Literacy in Education, Workplace and Everyday Contexts*. Oxford: Chandos Publishing, 2010.

Lupton, Mandy Jean. *The Learning Connection: Information Literacy and the Student Experience*. Blackwood: South Australia: Auslib Press, 2004.

Mackey, Thomas P., and Trudi E. Jacobson. *Metaliteracy: Reinventing Information Literacy to Empower Learners*. Chicago: Neal-Schuman, 2014.

Martin, Justine. "Refreshing Information Literacy." *Communications in Information Literacy* 7, no. 2 (2013): 114–27.

Meyer, Jan, and Ray Land. *Threshold Concepts and Troublesome Knowledge: Linkages to Ways of Thinking and Practicing within the Disciplines*. Edinburgh, UK: University of Edinburgh, 2003.

Meyer, Jan H. F., Ray Land, and Caroline Baillie. "Editors' Preface." In *Threshold Concepts and Transformational Learning*, edited by Jan H. F. Meyer, Ray Land, and Caroline Baillie, ix–xlii. Rotterdam, Netherlands: Sense Publishers, 2010.

Middendorf, Joan, and David Pace. "Decoding the Disciplines: A Model for Helping Students Learn Disciplinary Ways of Thinking." *New Directions for Teaching and Learning*, no. 98 (2004): 1–12.

Oakleaf, Megan. "A Roadmap for Assessing Student Learning Using the New Framework for Information Literacy for Higher Education." *Journal of Academic Librarianship* 40, no. 5 (September 2014): 510–4.

Secker, Jane. *A New Curriculum for Information Literacy: Expert Consultation Report*. Arcadia Project, Cambridge University Library, July 2011. http://ccfil.pbworks.com/f/Expert_report_final.pdf.

Townsend, Lori, Korey Brunetti, and Amy R. Hofer. "Threshold Concepts and Information Literacy." *portal: Libraries and the Academy* 11, no. 3 (2011): 853–69.

Tucker, Virginia, Christine Bruce, Sylvia Edwards, and Judith Weedman. "Learning Portals: Analyzing Threshold Concept Theory for LIS Education." *Journal of Education for Library and Information Science* 55, no. 2 (2014): 150–65.

Wiggins, Grant, and Jay McTighe. *Understanding by Design*. Alexandria, VA: Association for Supervision and Curriculum Development, 2004.

Recommended Reading

Banks, Marcus. "Time for a Paradigm Shift: The New ACRL Information Literacy Competency Standards for Higher Education." *Communications in Information Literacy* 7, no. 2 (2013): 184–188.

Brunetti, Korey, Amy R. Hofer, and Lori Townsend. "Interdisciplinarity and Information Literacy Instruction: A Threshold Concepts Approach." In *Threshold Concepts: From Personal Practice to Communities of Practice*, Proceedings of the National Academy's Sixth Annual Conference and the Fourth Biennial Threshold Concepts Conference, edited by C. O'Mahoney, A. Buchanan, M. O'Rourke, & B. Higgs, Cork, 89–93, Ireland: NAIRTL, 2014.

Cahoy, Ellysa Stern. "Affective Learning and Personal Information Management: Essential Components of Information Literacy." *Communications in Information Literacy* 7, no. 2 (2013): 146–149.

Hofer, Amy R., Korey Brunetti, and Lori Townsend. "A Threshold Concepts Approach to the Standards Revision." *Communications in Information Literacy* 7, no. 2 (2013): 108–113.

Hofer, Amy R., Lori Townsend, and Korey Brunetti. "Troublesome Concepts and Information Literacy: Investigating Threshold Concepts for IL Instruction." *portal : Libraries and the Academy* 12, no. 4, (2012): 387–405.

Ianuzzi, Patricia Anne. "Info lit 2.0 or Déjà Vu?" *Communications in Information Literacy* 7, no. 2 (2013): 98–107.

Jacobs, Heidi LM. "Minding the Gaps: Exploring the Space between Vision and Assessment in Information Literacy Work." *Communications in Information Literacy* 7, no. 2 (2013): 128–138.

Jacobson, Trudi E., and Thomas P. Mackey. "Proposing a Metaliteracy Model to Redefine Information Literacy." *Communications in Information Literacy* 7, no. 2 (2013): 84–91.

Kuhlthau, Carol C. "Rethinking the 2000 ACRL Standards: Some Things to Consider." *Communications in Information Literacy* 7, no. 2 (2013): 92–97.

Land, Ray, Glynis Cousin, Jan H.F. Meyer, and Peter Davies. "Threshold Concepts and Troublesome Knowledge: Implications for Course Design and Evaluation." In *Improving Student Learning: Diversity and Inclusivity*, Proceedings of the 12th Improving Student Learning Symposium, Birmingham, England, 2004, edited by Chris Rust, 2005.

Meyer, Jan. H.F. and Land, Ray. *Threshold Concepts and Troublesome Knowledge: Linkages to Ways of Thinking and Practising within the Disciplines.* Occasional Report 4. Enhancing Teaching-Learning Environments in Undergraduate Courses Project, Higher and Community Education, School of Education, University of Edinburgh: Scotland. http://www.colorado.edu/ftep/documents/ETLreport4-1.pdf

Land, Ray, Jan H.F. Meyer, and Jan Smith, eds. *Threshold Concepts with the Disciplines.* Boston: Sense Publishers, 2008.

Meyer, Jan, H.F., and Ray Land, eds. *Overcoming Barriers to Student Understanding: Threshold Concepts and Troublesome Knowledge.* New York: Routledge, 2006.

Meyer, Jan, H.F., Ray Land and Caroline Baillie, eds. *Threshold Concepts and Transformational Learning.* Boston: Sense Publishers, 2010.

Mackey, Thomas P., and Trudi E. Jacobson. "Reframing Information Literacy as a Metaliteracy." *College and Research Libraries* 72, no. 1 (2011): 62–78.

Martin, Justine. "Refreshing Information Literacy: Learning from Recent British Information Literacy Models." *Communications in Information Literacy* 7, no. 2 (2013): 114–127.

Seale, Maura. "Marketing Information Literacy." *Communications in Information Literacy* 7, no. 2 (2013): 154–160.

Townsend, Lori, Korey Brunetti, and Amy R. Hofer. "Threshold Concepts and Information Literacy." *portal : Libraries and the Academy* 11, no. 3, (2011): 853–869.

About the Editors

Gayle Schaub is the liaison librarian to the Art and Design, Modern Languages, and Psychology departments at Grand Valley State University Libraries. She holds an MLIS from the University of Wisconsin Milwaukee and an MA in Teaching English as a Foreign Language from the American University in Cairo. Gayle's other research interests include library services to international students and information literacy in K–12 education.

Hazel McClure is the liaison librarian to English, Writing, and Environmental Studies at Grand Valley State University. She holds an MFA from Saint Mary's College of California and an MLS from State University of New York at Buffalo. Her research interests are collaboration with disciplinary faculty, threshold concepts, and poetry publishing models.

Patricia Bravender is a professional programs librarian and liaison to Legal Studies, Criminal Justice, and Hospitality and Tourism Management at Grand Valley State University in Allendale, Michigan. She is also an adjunct faculty member in the School of Criminal Justice at GVSU where she supervises the internship programs in legal studies. She holds an MLIS from Wayne State University. In addition to threshold concepts, her research interests are information privacy and censorship.

Contributors

Todd Aldridge, English Graduate Teaching Assistant, Auburn University (Auburn, Alabama)

Dr. Smita Avasthi, Public Services and Lead Instruction Librarian, Santa Rosa Junior College (Santa Rose, California)

Andrea Baer, Undergraduate Education Librarian, Indiana University Bloomington (Bloomington, Indiana)

Rebecca Bliquez, Lead Librarian for Online Research & Instruction, Seattle University (Seattle, Washington)

Patricia Bravender, Professional Programs Librarian, Grand Valley State University (Allendale, Michigan)

Dani Brecher, Information Literacy and Learning Technologies Coordinator, Claremont Colleges Library (Claremont, California)

Melissa Browne, Instruction & Reference Librarian, University of California, Davis (Davis, California)

Richard Caldwell, Head of Library Instruction, University of California, Santa Barbara (Santa Barbara, California)

Toni M. Carter, Library Instruction Coordinator, Auburn University (Auburn, Alabama)

Rebecca Daly, Head Librarian, Finlandia University (Hancock, Michigan)

Ika Datig, Reference and Research Librarian, New York University, Abu Dhabi (Abu Dhabi, United Arab Emirates)

Robert Farrell, Assistant Professor, Library Coordinator of Information Literacy and Assessment, Lehman College, City University of New York (New York, New York)

Nancy Fawley, Head, Library Liaison Program, University of Nevada, Las Vegas (Las Vegas, Nevada)

Jenny Fielding, Reference Librarian, Northern Essex Community College (Haverhill, Massachusetts)

Emily Frigo, First Year Initiatives Coordinator, Grand Valley State University, (Allendale, Michigan)

Samantha Godbey, Education Librarian, Assistant Professor, University of Nevada, Las Vegas (Las Vegas, Nevada)

Xan Goodman, Health and Life Sciences Liaison Librarian, University of Nevada, Las Vegas (Las Vegas, Nevada)

Emily Hamstra, Learning Librarian, Kinesiology Librarian, University of Michigan, Ann Arbor (Ann Arbor, Michigan)

Steven Hoover, Learning Commons Librarian, Syracuse University Libraries (Syracuse, New York)

Charissa Jefferson, Business and Data Librarian, California State University, Northridge (Northridge, California)

Stephen "Mike," Kiel, Reference and Instruction Librarian, University of Baltimore (Baltimore, Maryland)

Keven Michael Klipfel, Information Literacy Coordinator, California State University, Chico (Chico, California)

Rebecca Kuglitsch, Interdisciplinary Science Librarian, University of Colorado, Boulder (Boulder, Colorado)

Kathleen Anne Langan, Humanities Librarian, Western Michigan University (Kalamazoo, Michigan)

Sami Lange, Public Services and Instruction Librarian, Santa Rose Junior College (Santa Rosa, California)

Melissa Langridge, User Education Coordinator, Niagara University (Lewiston, New York)

Melissa Mallon, Coordinator of Library Instruction, Wichita State University Libraries (Wichita, Kansas)

Elizabeth Martin, Head Librarian, Professional Programs, Grand Valley State University (Allendale, Michigan)

Hazel McClure, Liaison Librarian to English, Writing, and Environmental Studies, Grand Valley State University (Allendale, Michigan)

Rachel M. Minkin, Head of Reference Services, Michigan State University (East Lansing, Michigan)

Debbie Morrow, Liaison Librarian, Grand Valley State University (Allendale, Michigan)

Sarah Naumann, Literacy Program Coordinator, San Mateo Public Library (San Mateo, California); Adjunct Faculty, Library Instruction, California State University, East Bay (Hayward, California)

Jo Angela Oehrli, Learning Librarian, Children's Literature Librarian, University of Michigan (Ann Arbor, Michigan)

Cate Calhoun Oravet, Reference and Instruction Librarian, Auburn University (Auburn, Alabama)

Cathy Palmer, Education and Outreach Department Head, University of California Irvine (Irvine, California)

Caitlin Plovnick, First-Year Instruction and Outreach Librarian, Sonoma State University (Rohnert Park, California)

Pete Ramsey, Reference and Instruction Librarian, University of Baltimore (Baltimore, Maryland)

Jessalyn Richter, Writing Instructor, Grand Valley State University (Allendale, Michigan)

Gayle Schaub, Liberal Arts Librarian, Grand Valley State University (Allendale, Michigan)

Christopher Toth, Assistant Professor of Writing, Grand Valley State University (Allendale, Michigan)

Jane Van Galen, Professor, School of Education, University of Washington Bothell (Bothell, Washington)

Sue Wainscott, STEM Librarian, Assistant Professor, University of Nevada, Las Vegas (Las Vegas, Nevada)

Brandon West, Online Instruction/Instructional Design Librarian, State University of New York at Oswego (Oswego, New York)